6/96

S0-AZP-029

Dear David,

with much

love

MASTERING THE EUROMARKETS

A Guide to International Bonds: The Instruments, The Players and The Game

Valerie Thompson

Irwin Professional Publishing

London, England
Chicago, Illinois

First published in 1996 by
Irwin Professional Europe, Lynton House,
7-12 Tavistock Square, London WC1H 9LB

© 1996, Valerie E. Thompson

ALL RIGHTS RESERVED. No part of this publication may be reproduced, stored in a retrieval system, or transmitted in any form or by any means, electronic, photocopying, recording or otherwise, without the prior written permission of the publisher and the copyright holder.

Any statements and opinions expressed herein are published as a general guide for readers, but are not to be taken as recommendations by the publisher of any investment or course of action.

While every effort has been made to ensure the accuracy of information contained herein, the publisher accepts no liability for any errors or omissions.

This publication is designed to provide accurate and authoritative information in regard to the subject matter covered. It is sold with the understanding that the publisher is not engaged in rendering legal, accounting or other professional service.

Designed, illustrated and typeset by Nick Battley, London, England

ISBN 1 900717 00 X

Printed and bound in Great Britain by
Biddles Ltd, Guildford and King's Lynn

Acknowledgments

When I started thinking about all those who had helped in the production of this book, I realized it included all my colleagues at Salomon Brothers, my clients, and all the people in the market that I have met and worked with since founding Euromarket Trading Consultants Limited.

I especially want to thank Salomon Brothers for embracing, encouraging and supporting me throughout my career. In particular, I would like to thank Eddie Aronson for hiring me into the firm in 1973, and Michael Mortara for giving me the opportunity to trade, and for guiding me along the way. Charles S. McVeigh III was outstanding in his management of me, as was Ron Stuart and the late Bill Voute, all of whom offered unwavering faith.

I have drawn heavily on the help of friends and colleagues. For their particularly valuable suggestions, contributions, constructive criticism and encouragement, I am especially grateful to David Delucia, John Dowsett, Masayuki (Mark) Iijima, Sam Lusty, Tony Maude, Mark Mazzonelli, Alan McDougall, Gary McElroy, Simon Meadows, Peter Moles, Sandy Noble, Stephen Oristaglio, David Ovendon, Edward Reeves, Stanley Ross, David Schwartz and Oliver Weindling. All mistakes are naturally mine, and not theirs.

Much gratitude is also due to Nebille (Neil) Afram for his invaluable help and advice with the very first draft of this book, as well as the late Audrey Williamson for her outstanding secretarial support.

I would also like to thank Victoria Reeves for transforming the manuscript with her exceptional editing skills, Karen Wilkins for her invaluable assistance in the preparation of the glossaries and help with earlier drafts, and Oliver Wells and all others at Irwin for their enthusiasm of this project.

Last but not least, heaps of love and thanks to my precious children, Claire and Alex, for their understanding, patience and good humour.

London, March 1996   *Valerie Thompson*

Contents

Introduction

This book is based on first-hand experience of the eurobond markets. It contains everything I consider necessary to achieve success when trading and placing international securities. These markets involve the assessment of currencies, interest rates and credit, as well as diverse investor groups. The amounts traded can be as great as those found in any major domestic government market; single transactions of $50 million are not uncommon, though it is also possible to invest as little as $1,000. This is why the markets attract individual, as well as institutional, investors and a diverse range of borrowers including private companies, supranational organizations and governments, from both industrialized and developing regions.

I traded various international securities for Salomon Brothers—for whom I worked for nearly fourteen years—and for the last eight, have provided consulting, training and recruitment services to Street firms. I know therefore, what it takes to succeed within a major organization and also how other firms operate. Since leaving Salomon to set up my own company, I have learned much more about the Street in a broader context. For example, the way Street firms approach hiring and what they look for in a person, and what type of training various firms provide. I have also met hundreds of skilled personnel and discussed career-related issues, and have naturally, along the way, learned a great deal more about individual perspectives. All of this has proven invaluable in writing this book.

When I started work on the trading floor, there was a great deal I did not understand both conceptually and mathematically. Yet I could not find any book that made sense to me, or which explained all the pieces of the 'euromarket' (as the market for international securities is commonly known) jigsaw, and how they fitted together. While there were plenty of books available on bond mathematics, this is only one aspect of the business. In any event, the mathematical books recommended were of little use, since I did not have the academic background to be able to understand all the formulae.

This book is in many ways therefore, the antithesis of an academic textbook, in that it focuses on the practicalities involved in the trading and placing of international securities. Every key aspect of trading and sales is covered, from the thought processes involved in assessing markets and servicing clients, to practical examples showing that assessment and service in practice. There is also a step-by-step guide to international bond market instruments, and the calculations used to assess their value. In addition, there is information and calculations on many other products, i.e. the money markets, the derivative markets and certain government markets. Coverage of these areas is necessary because eurobond traders constantly make comparisons with other products and markets in order to assess the attractiveness of their own.

They may also use another market to protect (hedge) themselves against adverse interest rate movements. There is, for instance, no 'eurobond futures contract'. Eurobond traders therefore, often use the relevant government futures markets to hedge their eurobond positions. A eurobond transaction may also involve a foreign exchange and/or interest rate swap and, if it is a very short-dated eurobond, may also require comparison with similar instruments in the money markets. All these areas are covered. In short, I have attempted to include everything I feel a trader or salesperson of international securities should know in order to be effective in their work.

Whilst this book is essentially a practical guide for newcomers to the business, it is also designed to be a 'refresher' for established practitioners, particularly those who have not had the benefit of any formal training. The grids and checklists, more valuable for their time efficiency than their technical content, are still of use to me today. The mathematical chapters are designed for those who find this aspect of the business as hard as I did, and aim to demystify, as well as inculcate an intuitive grasp of where prices and yields ought to be.

All formulae are followed by examples, workable with the most basic of calculators. One that has just the basic functions, is all you will need. I make no apologies for stating the obvious or including simple checklists, as I have enough experience to know how much money can be lost as a result of a simple mistake and/or a lack of basic discipline. Given the speed with which decisions have to be made, common sense and procedure are often abandoned when it matters most.

When I started in this business, there were a limited number of products and participants. This changed dramatically during the '80s when many new firms entered the arena and the markets experienced unprecedented growth. Aided by both the technology to compute complex calculations quickly, and deregulation (the relaxation of regulations governing the flow of money around the world), the markets attracted a host of new borrowers and gave birth to a variety of products with more complex structures. The international bond markets now boast more players, more products, more markets, and more competition than ever before. Consequently, I believe there is a need for a clear, common-sense guide that explains them from both a human, and technical, standpoint. Whether I have created as much, is for the reader to judge.

To be successful in any industry it is not necessary to know or do it all. Just to know and do more than the rest. To achieve long-term success in the markets, there is much to learn and a lot to do. The unique combination of skills, experience and common sense required to reach the top should not be under-estimated. Talent alone is not enough. A sense of responsibility and stamina for sheer hard work are equally important.

The intensity of a dealing environment and the speed with which information must be assimilated and acted upon, requires lightning reactions and a strong stomach. The markets are intensely competitive and comprise some very sharp minds. Focus, staying power, persistence, and a desire to win intelligently are essential traits. And while there may be a minority who are more arrogant than is justified, the majority think more about what they do not know than what they do know, and care more about what they can give to this business than what they can get from it.

Readers who are totally new to the markets may find certain sections of this book a little complicated. Do not spend time trying to digest information and concepts that are not yet relevant or useful. When they do make more sense, which they will with the benefit of more experience, simply re-read them at that time.

This book contains a lot of glossaries. There is one at the beginning of most chapters and a complete glossary at the end. As you will need to understand 'Street-speak' it is essential to read the glossary at the beginning of a chapter before proceeding to read the chapter itself. Terms explained in a preceding glossary are not repeated and so the glossaries become progressively shorter in later chapters.

Lastly, I intend no offence by using the term 'he' rather than 's/he'. Being female, some may feel it appropriate for me to use 'she'. But the financial markets comprise far more men than women and it seems sensible to accommodate the majority.

.

Chapter 1

2

GLOSSARY FOR CHAPTER 1

arbitrage
To arbitrage is to buy and sell the same or similar securities to take advantage of price discrepancies.

bond
Technically known as a 'certificate of indebtedness' or debt instrument, because it is a debt obligation of the issuer (borrowing entity). Bond, issue, deal and security are synonymous terms and therefore interchangeable in 'Street speak', e.g., when requesting a price for a bond issued by Marks & Spencer one might say: "Where is the M & S bond?"; "How is the M & S deal?"; "Where is the M & S issue trading?"; "What is the price of the M & S security?". One would of course qualify this further if there were two or more securities outstanding.

house
A financial institution involved in the securities industry. *See* **Street (The)** below.

investor
An entity or individual that buys and sells securities for investment rather than speculation. These include pension funds, insurance companies and fund managers. Investors are also known as *clients*, *institutional investors*, *retail accounts* or simply just *accounts*, or simply just *retail*, although some firms reserve the use of the term retail to describe individual, rather than institutional, investors.

proprietary
A firm that acts in a proprietary capacity uses its own capital, i.e. money which belongs to its principals or partners or, in the case of a public corporation, its shareholders.

relative value
Of value as compared to alternative similar services and products.

Street (The)
Derived from 'Wall Street'. A generic term used to describe the collective business of financial institutions involved in the securities industry, i.e. firms that intermediate between users (borrowers) and lenders (investors) of money, often trading (buying and selling) securities for their own account, as well as on behalf of institutional investors.

❖

Chapter 1

Street life

The Street is in many ways a free for all, a jungle where only the fittest survive. But it continues to attract the talented and ambitious, being one of the few industries to provide intellectual stimulation and challenge, well-above-average financial rewards, and an exciting fast-paced atmosphere.

The characters

We all have our quirks and particular ways of expressing ourselves, and the Street comprises a rich mixture of personalities, some of whom communicate in bizarre ways. Puerile and tasteless comments can abound, and you will need to develop a mentally-robust disposition to survive. If easily shocked or unable to tolerate profanities, this business is not for you. When vast sums of money are at risk and decisions have to be made in split seconds, swearing and shouting are some of the more common ways for traders and salespeople to relieve stress and deal with panic. The Street comprises a fairly even mix of academics and those who worked their way up as I did. The arrogant, the humble, the generous, the greedy, the extrovert and the introvert can all be found.

Success traits

Success will depend on the ability to do a job, which, it is critical to note, includes being able to communicate with different cultures and personalities from diverse social backgrounds. Do not underestimate the importance of communication skills. I have seen more people fail due to an inability to communicate and/or work as a member of a team, than from lack of education and/or innate money-making skills. Individual prejudices and preferences aside, those who can do a job well and can fit in, stand the best chance of achieving success in all its forms.

While a good education may secure an interview and enable you to grasp concepts and tackle the mathematics of the business more easily, your long-term success will depend far more on an ability to deal with people. By the same token, while an instinctive ability to make money may get you a job, keeping it and progressing up the career ladder, will depend on how you treat others. If you can 'produce' and handle all other aspects of a job well, you will be in demand.

Quality of life

Those wanting a long and happy career in the markets, need to create their own ground rules. Work out what you want from life, both personally and professionally, and decide what you are prepared to give to your career. If not, you could find yourself a victim of the system. As you get older, your values may change, but unless you have a core set of values at the outset in terms of what you will and will not do, both physically and morally, other people will decide for you and in turn dictate your destiny. If you do not control life, life will control you. Just remember, the Street's priority is to make money—not to consider your long-term welfare. That is your responsibility and it is no different in any other industry.

Pay and staff turnover

Disparities in pay are widespread and there tends to be an inverse correlation between age and pay. A relatively young trader or salesperson can earn much more than older colleagues.

Firms have two main choices when deciding to expand. They can 'grow their own' talent or buy it in. Because organic growth takes time and is often not feasible, many firms implant skills and experience by hiring specialists from competitors to gain a foothold in a market quickly. Young rising stars with approximately three to five years' experience, who can be lured away fairly easily with the bait of more money, are often the target group.

Due to the proliferation of both products and dealing firms over the last fifteen years, there continues to be a shortage of experienced people with the precise skills, track record and disposition required. Losing staff can therefore be a major headache for a firm. Finding replacement staff can take a few months, and it can then take a few more months for a new employee to understand their organization and 'gel' with existing staff. In the meantime, a firm can lose market share and more critically, miss out on numerous money-making opportunities. To lose just one employee can erode a firm's competitive edge, but to lose a number can destroy its presence in a market completely.

One way some firms endeavour to keep their best producers, is to pay them a hard-cut of the profits they generate, although for trading staff, this approach is usually limited to proprietary traders rather than market-makers. Proprietary traders speculate with their firm's capital and do not usually get involved in customer business. It is therefore easier to assess their contribution to profits. Deals like this can be very sweet, particularly as they tend to be structured so that a trader only shares in the upside, i.e. does not suffer in any way if he loses, rather than makes, money. Such preferential treatment for a select few individuals within an otherwise large organization can, of course, be divisive and cause a lot of resentment. However, for companies with a limited budget for recruitment, it is a route via which they can attract talented people and, in turn, increase their chances of making big money.

Do bear in mind, however, that while the lure of a hard-cut—or simply more money in general—can be tempting, there are risks in giving up the security of an environment in which you have proven your worth and where you are known and have proven to be a survivor. You should also take into account that, by changing jobs too frequently, your lack of loyalty could make it harder to find work when it matters most. Furthermore, by demanding too much money, you could price yourself out of the market, especially during a period of contraction and redundancies, of which this industry has seen many.

I would also discourage you from joining a firm that is prepared to pay a ridiculous amount of money. In my experience, companies pay in direct proportion to their lack of understanding about what it takes to build a successful operation. By joining such a firm, you, too, could become a casualty of their incompetence—sooner rather than later. It is worth bearing in mind that, generally speaking, a house that is willing to hire on a purely economic basis will also fire on a purely economic basis. Remember, too, that big bucks can be achieved as much through tenure as from job-hopping.

Continuity

Staying with a firm can aid your maturity, improve your strategic skills, and, in turn, increase your value in the marketplace. If you always get going when the going gets tough, you may miss out on the type of experiences that can breed richness of character and wisdom, and from which you can learn management skills, if only by witnessing how *not* to handle situations!

If disgruntled and feeling like a change, no doubt you will be able to come up with reasons to support a move to another house. But there are risks in moving: I have met many people who changed their jobs only to find, once the honeymoon period was over, that the firm they joined was no better and, in some cases, was actually worse than the one they left.

Although a situation can arise wherein a person's contribution is undervalued by an employer to such an extent that leaving is the best option, this is the exception rather than the rule. Most grievances and problems can be sorted out without resorting to resignation. When experiencing difficulties, which we all do from time to time, I would encourage you to seek solutions rather than look for an alternative place of work. Moreover, as far as personalities and practices are concerned, you are unlikely to find any better or any worse, wherever you work. While the faces and names may be different, the politics and games will be much the same. Different clowns, same circus, so to speak.

The recruitment process

There is no real science to the Street's recruitment process. Some firms make a decision having met an applicant two or three times, whilst others may want ten interviews and meetings with thirty to forty members of staff. There is not necessarily any correlation between the length of the interviewing process and your chances of success. The firm that wants you to meet forty people may not be more scientific in their approach to hiring. Indeed, they may be far less able to reach a decision since they allow too many people to influence the outcome. In any event, when attending an interview make sure that you treat every interviewer you meet with respect, and be sure to thank them for the time they have given—even if an interviewer is discourteous or difficult.

Assessing a potential employer

Contrary to popular opinion, some firms lack the courage to fire people who are not producing results. Because some managers find it hard to confront the lazy and/or incompetent, many simply wait for them to get the message and leave of their own volition. Not surprisingly, this tends to result in the best producers getting disenchanted and leaving, while the weak and needy hang on. Forewarned is forearmed. Before joining a firm, be satisfied that it is at least as good, preferably better, than your existing firm. Check that it has proven its commitment and know-how in other markets, and find out what its level of staff turnover has been. Try to establish how many people have left recently, at least during the previous year, and why, bearing in mind that high staff turnover destroys morale internally, and erodes credibility among borrowers and investors. And remember, if offered a job after one interview, you should feel more concerned than flattered. The way a firm approaches recruitment is a good indicator of its culture and philosophy. A firm that is either desperate or slapdash, is equally worrying.

If your priority is job security and financial reward, look to join a profitable group within a profitable firm, run by an individual who commands respect and from whom you can learn. Although you will ideally want to work within a happy, friendly group, this should be a secondary consideration because, unless a team produces good results, it will fall apart—and sooner, rather than later. Whilst I know from experience that it is possible for a group of people to work happily and effectively together, it is not to be looked for in the ordinary course of events. If a potential employer says that everyone gets along like a house on fire, be sceptical. Mutual admiration societies and happy chatter will not pay your bonus or secure your career.

Big firm or small firm?

While there are merits to working for a small firm, unless you already have a lot of experience there needs to be a critical mass of experienced superiors already in place for you to continue learning. If a small firm appeals because it represents an opportunity to become a bigger fish in a small pond, do take into account that your learning curve could come to an abrupt halt. By joining a small firm while still young, with no others from whom to learn, you could be the one everyone else looks to for advice. That said, one can learn an enormous amount working in a small firm that has a core of experienced people and a cohesive strategy. Moreover, it can be great fun. There were eight people at Salomon Brothers in London in 1973 when I joined the firm. I never looked back.

Power and influence

The securities industry is more meritocratic and short-term than most. It rewards profitability with power, regardless of age. Good, but young, producers are often promoted to managers, though few receive any management training. This business is not about structure, methodology or considered forethought. It is about making money. The stakes can be enormous. Greed, fear and self-preservation dominate, and survival depends on winning more times than you lose.

During your career you will encounter people whom you do not consider worthy of their status and/or influence. However, until you rise to the point where you also have power, it is better to keep your negative thoughts about a person to yourself. I have met more than one unemployed person who has complained bitterly about how unfair this business is and how useless his bosses were, etc. But their boss(es) still had jobs—they did not!

This is not to say that if a colleague, or even a superior, acts in an unscrupulous way, you should do nothing. Given the potential rewards available in this business, a lot of bluff and double-bluff can occur.

Someone with good self-marketing skills but little integrity, who is more slippery than smart, could certainly trick their way in. Needless to say, you should immediately report anyone whom you know to be acting in a way that could damage the fortunes and credibility of their employer. Do be sure, however, that you are operating on fact and not hearsay. The long-term health of the industry depends on its integrity. We all, therefore, have an obligation to look out for each other.

Management

Complaints about management abound in this business, and second-guessing is part of Street life. Fortunes can, and do, change quickly. A severe loss is often followed by a brief post-mortem and then an internal restructuring involving a change of management. In hindsight, changes often prove to be ghastly mistakes, but this happens in many industries. Because many managers are untrained, and also required to 'produce' as well as manage, they lack the time and know-how to deal with the various concerns of subordinates. They tend, therefore, to be blamed for everything from spilt coffee to earthquakes—notwithstanding that some complaints may be justified. It is easy, of course, to find flaws in the way any firm is managed because it is human nature to more readily see what is wrong, rather than what is right. Your working life, however, will be more pleasant and rewarding, if you concentrate on what is right about management or an individual manager, rather than only what is wrong.

Politics and gossip

There are as many opinions as there are people in this business. Never 'badmouth' anyone or any firm, particularly colleagues, bosses or employers in general. It is not good business practice and you never know when your paths will next cross. By the same token, do not be too influenced by others' tales, and avoid forming an opinion on half a story. There are always two sides, sometimes twenty-two, to each story and most get embellished in the telling. Of course office politics exist, but there is such a thing as divine justice. We get back what we give out. It is almost as if there were a precise law of cause and effect.

Be sure, therefore, that your motives are *con*structive rather than *de*structive. Always work in the best interests of your employer, rather than yourself, or at the least your employer first and yourself second. Not the other way around. Operate on the basis that organizations have a thousand ears and that anything said about anyone will get back to that person. Try to be your own counsel, get on with your job and avoid the politics. You will find that Street life exposes characters in all their splendour and ugliness. It is hard to hide. I think this is because, on any one day, so many diverse and risky situations can arise that must be dealt with immediately. This leaves little time to censor our actions and reactions, which is why, I believe, our true nature is exposed sooner rather than later.

Envy

Do not talk about how much money you earn. The concept of wealth is appealing to everyone, but the amounts of money paid to individuals in this business can, and do, cause envy. In all walks of life, whoever has the most is generally envied by some. Life never seems fair to the have-nots, who regard themselves as such by looking only at those better off, rather than those worse off than themselves. Success to the unsuccessful is generally attributed to luck, rather than effort, because it supports their own excuses and reasons for not having achieved much, or as much. It is the same in the Street. There is little to gain and much to lose by telling friends and/or colleagues what you earn. It is nobody's business but your own.

Losses

The FRN market crisis (1986/87), the stock market crash (1987), 'Black Wednesday' in the gilt market and the Ecu market crisis (1992) are a few instances of sophisticated financial institutions losing vast sums of money from trading activities, although the collapse of Barings Bank (1995) is by far the best example of what can go wrong.

Errors of judgement can and do occur, more so if there are no ground rules and basic disciplines in place. While costly events beyond an individual's or an entire firm's control do occur from time to time, a lot of money can also be lost through general tardiness and a lack of cohesion. For example, a firm that allows employees to work to different agendas and operate with individual—rather than firm-wide—disciplines, is far more likely to experience losses. However, by remembering your responsibilities toward your employer and endeavouring to fulfill your obligations as an employee, you are less likely to lose money. This would include focusing more on what you could lose for your employer, rather than what you could make for them in any given situation. When trading, never lose sight of the fact that you are dealing with someone else's money, or that a very, very big loss can start with just one person.

The Street's relative value

No industry can survive without takers for its products and/or services, and if the Street did not have a role to play, it would not exist. The capital it commits, the products it creates, and the services it provides, increase the options available to both users and lenders of money. As a provider of capital, the Street often offers better terms than can be achieved elsewhere. And for those with money to invest, the range of products available is vast, with yields that often surpass those available from traditional investments.

Of particular value, is the Street's role as the middle-man, whereby it commits its own capital in order to plug the time-gaps that often exist between the availability of, and the need for, money. Using financial engineering techniques, the Street can convert virtually any currency and asset structure so as to better match supply with demand.

The Street thrives on differences in the supply of, and demand for, money, and has created access and outlets for it, which would be hard for any individual entity to find directly. The Street's continued success, attests to it being both needed, and having a relative value.

Chapter 2

GLOSSARY FOR CHAPTER 2

bearer
The name of the owner of a 'bearer' bond is not registered, i.e. does not appear anywhere on the certificate that represents ownership. Bearer bond certificates are issued with interest coupons attached which owners clip off and simply present for payment. Coupon interest is therefore paid to the 'bearer' of the coupon.

capital markets
The markets where capital is raised. These include all the, domestic as well as international, markets.

Federal Reserve
The central bank of the United States, comprising a collection of banks, each of which is responsible for banking activities for a particular district, and all of which report to the Federal Reserve Board.

IPMA
International Primary Markets Association.

ISMA
International Securities Market Association.

offshore
Not domestic or home-based, i.e. markets or funds which are outside the control of the country represented by the currency in question.

OPEC
Oil Producing Exporting Countries.

primary market
The market for new issues.

SEC
Securities and Exchange Commission, a regulatory body (USA).

secondary market
The market where securities are traded after their initial launch and distribution, when they are no longer new issues.

SFA

The Securities and Futures Authority, a self-regulatory organization (SRO) in the UK.

SIB

Securities and Investments Board, the head of a group of regulatory bodies set up to regulate investment businesses and to protect investors.

Chapter 2

Background

The international securities markets, of which the eurobond markets represent the largest sector, comprise some 20,000 securities denominated in thirty different currencies, representing a nominal amount equivalent to around US$2250 billion. The turnover in 1995 was around US$32,500 billion![1]

These markets originated in Europe, but are now traded in all major financial centres around the world. Consequently, eurobonds are now known as international securities. 'Euro' has been replaced with 'international', and 'bond' has been replaced with 'securities', as it can be used to describe a variety of instruments including, but not restricted to, bonds. Rather than talking in terms of eurobonds traded in the euromarkets, it is now more appropriate to talk in terms of international bonds traded in the international securities markets. However, I have used the terms eurobond and euromarkets throughout this book as they are still the most commonly used descriptions.

The attraction of eurobonds

The eurobond markets are 'offshore' markets. A sort of second home for securities issued outside the control of the domestic authorities by which the currency of denomination would normally be governed. This means they cannot, for example, be frozen as a result of an international dispute, because no one country has control over them.

Eurobonds are issued in bearer as opposed to registered form, which protects the identity of investors. In the early years of the market's growth, Swiss investors, who loved the anonymity aspect, and the high-grade European and US issuers that the market attracted, accounted for probably 80 per cent of investor demand. Interest is also free of withholding tax,

---

[1] *Figures taken from the ISMA's 'Handbook of Statutes, By-laws, Rules and Recommendations', January 1996.*

which means investors receive their interest payments in full, as opposed to having a portion withheld as tax, and then having to claim it back.

Eurobond issuance procedures are also relatively simple and quick. Transactions involving complex structures are commonplace and vast sums (single transactions of one billion US$ or the equivalent are quite common) can be raised in virtually any actively-traded currency.

London is the world's largest centre for the issuance of eurobonds. Frankfurt is second and, to a lesser extent—but growing in importance—there is Paris, Milan, Hong Kong and Singapore.

Eurobonds are, however, traded on a secondary basis throughout the world.

There is no difference between a euro currency and a domestic currency except for ownership. For example, a US dollar becomes an 'international' or 'euro' dollar when it is held offshore in a foreign bank account, because it is then outside the control of the US banking authorities.

A brief history

The eurodollar bond markets were created to take advantage of large amounts of dollars held in Europe following World War II, when the US dollar replaced sterling as the main trading currency. As a result of the Bretton Woods Agreement (1944), when European countries agreed to maintain fixed values for their currencies, US dollars were sought after as a reserve currency which could be sold by European central banks to support their own currencies in a crisis. The Cold War also aided the build up of dollars in Europe as Communist central banks transferred their dollar assets to avoid them being frozen by the US Government. Various capital controls, imposed by the US during the '60s in an attempt to deal with their balance of payments deficit, also helped, particularly the Interest Equalization Tax introduced in 1963. IET penalized foreign borrowers with a tax on dollar funds raised in the US domestic market, which encouraged use of the international markets for dollar financing. The first eurodollar bond was issued in 1963.

The growth of bond markets in currencies other than US dollars, commonly known as the 'non-dollar' or 'euro-currency' bond markets', started in the 60's. It took hold however, during the 1970s when the US dollar was weak and sold in favour of stronger European currencies. Many of the dollars held by OPEC for example, were switched into European currencies and invested in bonds denominated in those currencies. The introduction of the European Monetary System in 1979 which links certain European currencies to each other and to the Ecu, and limits their movements within prescribed bands, provided more stability and aided the growth of euro currency bond markets. The first euro-Deutschemark, euroguilder and euro-French franc bonds were issued between 1965 and 1967.

To summarize, eurobonds cannot be frozen as a result of an international dispute, they are free from withholding tax, and investors in them can remain anonymous. The markets are also renowned for introducing new structures, and bonds can be issued simply and speedily and in vast amounts. For these reasons, the growth of the international bond markets over the last 30 years has been phenomenal, making them the most free and innovative sector of all the world's capital markets. This does not mean however, that they are unpoliced.

Regulation

All operators must comply with the regulatory authorities in the country/city/state in which they operate. They will also naturally want to uphold the same ethical standards with which they run their domestic operations, and endeavour to conduct their activities in ways consistent with domestic regulations. For example, a US investment bank in London must conduct its operations in accordance with the rules and regulations imposed by the UK's SIB (Securities and Investment Board). It will also, secondarily, want to run its business in ways satisfactory to the SEC in the United States (Securities and Exchange Commission).

For example, when I worked at Salomon Brothers, even though I was based in London and traded international securities, as opposed to domestic securities such as US Treasuries, I was still required to take various US exams. These included the NASD (National Association of Securities Dealers) Series 7 exam and, when the firm merged with commodity giant Phibro in 1981, the CFTC (Commodity Futures Trading Commission) exam.

The international markets also have numerous self-regulatory bodies. For the bond markets there is the International Securities Market Association (ISMA). This was founded in 1969 and formerly called the Association of International Bond Dealers, before changing its name in 1992. ISMA handles all matters relating to the 'secondary' trading and settlement of international securities, while the International Primary Market Association (IPMA) deals with the 'primary' market. Although both associations are non-regulatory bodies, they were created by the market for the market, to ensure against unethical practices or activities that could dilute the market's credibility and integrity. Their guidelines and recommendations are therefore treated seriously.

Regulation of the financial services industry is complex, and each country has its own regulatory framework and examinations. Commercial banking activities in the UK tend to be regulated by the Bank of England, whilst investment banking activities are regulated by the SFA. The SFA is a self-regulatory organization (SRO) assisted by the SIB. Other SROs include IMRO (Investment Management Regulatory Organization) and the PIA (Personal Investment Authority).

If you would like to know more about the UK regulatory system, the SIB publishes some very good booklets. I would also recommend that you read the handbooks issued by ISMA and IPMA which contain details of all rules and recommendations relating to the issuance, trading and settlement of international securities. For more information about the history of the markets, I would suggest *Eurobonds* by F.G. Fisher III. Details of all these publications can be found in the Bibliography.

Chapter 3

GLOSSARY FOR CHAPTER 3

accrued
Accrued interest. The build-up of interest between interest payment dates.

CD
Certificate of deposit. Issued by commercial banks against money held on deposit.

clearance
The exchange of securities for cash, or vice versa, in completion of a trade. Also known as *settlement*.

commercial paper
Unsecured short-term (less than one year) obligations, issued mostly by corporations and financial organizations.

coupon
The rate of interest payable on a security by the issuer.

derivative market
The market for financial products which are based on other products and/or markets, having been 'derived' from them. These include futures, options and warrants. A derivative instrument is always based on some other underlying security or market and cannot exist independently.

EBRD
European Bank for Reconstruction and Development.

higher repayment ranking
Bonds issued by banks usually rank *pari passu* (equal to) depositors, meaning that in the event of a default bondholders will be in the first category of debtors to be repaid.

IBRD
International Bank for Reconstruction and Development, also known as the World Bank.

inventory
Securities held in position.

Libid
London interbank bid rate, i.e. the interest rate at which banks will buy money from other banks, or what they will pay for deposits of money.

Libor
London interbank offered rate, i.e. the rate at which banks will lend (offer) money to other banks.

liquidity
Ease of tradeability of a security, i.e. the ease with which a security can be bought or sold. If there are a lot of dealers in a particular bond, then it is considered to be very liquid. If there are none, it would be illiquid.

M & A
Mergers and acquisitions.

maturity date
The date when a loan or security becomes due for redemption.

money market
As well as referring to the various markets that deal with deposits and loans of cash, it is the general term used to describe markets in short dated securities that are substitutes for cash, such as commercial paper (CP).

MTNs
Medium-term notes.

on-lend
Refers to borrowings of securities or funds that are then lent on to another entity/person.

OTC
An abbreviation for *over-the-counter*, i.e. the trading of securities that does not take place via a public exchange, such as the London Stock Exchange. OTC securities, which are usually traded by telephone or electronic screen, are not subject to the standardization of exchange-traded contracts and, in many cases, their terms may be negotiated by the parties to the trade.

par value
Refers to par or face value which is the principal amount (value) that appears on the face of a bond certificate, and upon which interest is calculated. Bonds are usually issued in denominations (with a face value) of 1000 or multiples thereof. When used in the context of bond prices therefore, par means 100 per cent of a principal amount of 1000 or some multiple of it. This is the amount an issuer will repay at maturity when they extinguish a debt obligation. Also note, that while coupons (interest payments), are based on par or face value, a security's real value—the price at which it can be bought or sold at a given time—will be a function of market conditions and

may be very different from face value. With regard to the stock market, par means the price assigned by a company to its common stock or ordinary shares.

perpetuals
Securities, such as FRNs, that have no maturity, or either a very long maturity, i.e. 99 years.

principal
The face amount, i.e. the initial loan to an issuer, which is repaid at maturity.

redemption
Expiration of a debt obligation. This is usually on a date that is set at the time a bond is issued, i.e. the maturity date. A borrower can redeem securities, and in so doing extinguish some or all of an outstanding debt obligation, through purchases in the secondary market prior to the official maturity date. Issuers sometimes do this if their securities are on sale at less than face, or redemption value, and if they can afford it.

repo
An abbreviation for repurchase agreement, comprising a simultaneous sale and buy back of securities. *See* Chapter 13.

settlement
See **clearance** above. Settlement is effected when securities and cash in respect of a transaction have been exchanged.

subordinated debt
Subordinated debt has a lower repayment ranking. In the event of a default therefore, senior noteholders would be paid before subordinated noteholders.

T-bills
Treasury bills. Short-term debt obligations of the US Government.

YTM
An abbreviation for *yield-to-maturity*. For a fixed-rate bond, this is the annual rate of return, based on its coupon, maturity and price, expressed as a percentage interest rate. *See* **yield** in the Glossary for Chapter 6.

Chapter 3

Products and participants: An overview

A bond is a security with a maturity longer than one year, and may also be called a *note*. Securities with maturities shorter than one year are, technically, money market instruments. However, there are numerous instruments that are neither strictly money-market instruments or bonds/notes, but a combination of both. Euro floating-rate notes (FRNs) for example, or a hybrid, such as euro medium-term notes (EMTNs). Innovation has created a variety of structures that fall between two stools, and the category into which a security belongs is frequently blurred. Also note, that the term 'eurobond' is used loosely to describe a broad range of securities including traditional fixed-rate eurobonds, euro-FRNs and euro-zeros.

The structure of bonds

The technical description of a bond is 'debt certificate', so-called because it is essentially an IOU. The price paid for a bond, incorporates a loan to the issuer of a principal amount, upon which interest income is received. Interest income is also known as *coupon income* (*see* Glossary). Eurobonds, FRNs and zeros are all bonds, though each has a different name due to a difference in structure. All however, are made up of principal and/or interest. Indeed, in the US, the interest and principal portions of a bond are often traded separately. What is called a US Treasury strip, is the interest cashflow on the underlying principal amount of a US government bond, while the principal-only portion, is the equivalent of a zero-coupon bond.

Traditional eurobonds pay a fixed rate of interest annually throughout their life. Floating-rate notes pay a variable or floating rate of interest which is reset (and paid) usually in relation to Libor, at regular intervals throughout their life, usually every three or six months. Zero-coupon bonds compound annually, but do not pay any interest during their life. The interest component is instead paid out in one lump sum at maturity. Zeros are issued at a discount and redeemed at par, the extent of the discount being a function of the yield, e.g. a 10-year zero will cost 38.55 if it is to yield 10 per cent. 38.55 compounded annually at 10 per cent for 10 years will produce 100 (prices and yields are explained in more detail later on).

To avoid confusion, I should also point out the key difference between traditional bonds of the aforementioned type, and convertible bonds. A convertible bond contains an embedded option which entitles the holder to convert the security into equity for a given price at certain times during the bond's life. To compensate (the issuer) for including (writing) this option, the coupon on a convertible bond is invariably lower than on a conventional bond, which means that holders, in lieu of their opportunity to convert, will not receive as much interest income. A convertible bond is therefore a hybrid security, that starts out as a debt instrument but which could end up as equity. As the price movement of convertibles tends to be more influenced by changes in the issuer's stock price than changes in interest rates, they are regarded more as equity than debt instruments.

To reiterate, all securities are made up of principal and/or interest. Remember this fact, as it will make it easier for you to follow the mathematical sections in this book.

The price of bonds

In addition to a principal amount, which is repaid up to par (face value) when a bond matures,[1] the price at which a bond is bought or sold will also reflect any difference between the stated coupon (rate of interest payable) and interest rates prevailing at the time of the transaction. Therefore, a government bond with a 10 per cent coupon and two years remaining to maturity will cost you more than par to purchase, if prevailing 2-year interest rates are lower than 10 per cent, and less than par if they are higher than 10 per cent (more about prices and yields later).

Interest calculations

Calculation of interest payments on bonds varies. Eurobonds only pay 360 days interest per year regardless of the fact that either 365 or 366 days will have lapsed. FRNs on the other hand, pay interest on actual days lapsed. Eurobonds also assume that each month comprises 30 days, regardless of the fact that some have 31 or that February only has 28. When buying or selling a security part way through an interest period, it is crucial to understand how accrued interest (which is payable to the seller) is

---

[1] *If, prior to the official maturity date, a bond is callable from the investor by the issuer, or puttable by the investor to the issuer, then the redemption price may be more or less than par.*

calculated, as this will affect the proceeds of a transaction. It is equally important to understand the basis upon which interest is calculated on money borrowed to finance the purchase of a security.

International bond prices are quoted net of accrued interest, i.e. if you receive a quote of par and you buy or sell bonds at that price, the settlement proceeds will be more than 100 per cent of face value if the bond is part way through an interest period, as accrued interest will be added to the price.

Methods of evaluation

There are numerous methods one can use to measure the value of a security. The yield-to-maturity concept (YTM, also known as *yield*) is the most common for fixed-income instruments, such as eurobonds, while for FRNs the 'discount margin' method is the norm. Both methods involve assumptions. The yield of a security is only a theoretical measure of value. Only once a security is sold or it matures, can one work out the total rate of return actually achieved over the holding period.

This book focuses on methods of evaluation and practices that have become universally accepted by the market. It does not attempt to assess the merits of one mathematical method over another. My aim has been to show readers how things are done, not to question why they are done a particular way. I think you will find the various conventions used to be relatively simple, perhaps too simple, for the more quantitative minds. However, for something to become a common standard, it needs to be simple enough for the majority of users to both understand and calculate. An uncomplicated standardized approach provides a starting point for everyone. A basic model via which people can compare like with like, and which can be modified to suit individual needs and preferences.

Market instruments

Market instruments fall into four main categories, as follows:

---

1. EQUITY MARKET

Main instruments	Usual issuers	Special features
Common stock or ordinary shares	Corporations/banks	Dividend payments paid on profit performance.
Preferred stock	Corporations/banks	Regular fixed dividend payment. Ranks slightly above common stock.
Convertibles	Corporations/banks	Fixed coupon, but the right to convert to equity at a later date.

| Bonds with equity warrants | Corporations/banks | Debt instrument with a warrant (see below) attached that gives holder the right to buy equity. |

Note: While a money or bond market instrument is akin to an IOU issued by a company, bank or country, stocks or shares represent a piece of a company.

2. MONEY MARKET

Main instruments	**Usual issuers**	**Special features**
Treasury bills (T-bills)	Governments	Issued and traded at a discount from redemption price.
Commercial paper (CP)	Corporations	Issued and traded at a discount from redemption price.
Certificates of deposit (CDs)	Banks	Issued and traded on a yield-to-maturity (YTM) basis.
Medium-term notes (MTNs)	Corporations/banks/ governments/gov't agencies	Pay fixed coupon. Issued on 'tap' basis. Because issuing procedure is similar to CDs and rotation can be as short as one year, this product falls into both the money and bond market categories.

3. BOND MARKET

Main instruments	**Usual issuers**	**Special features**
Bonds	Corporations/banks/building societies/governments/ government agencies	Pay fixed coupon. Higher repayment ranking than equity.
Floating -rate notes	Banks/building societies/governments/ government agencies	Pay refixed floating coupon, usually in relation to Libor (London interbank offered rate) Maturities extend to eternity in the case of perpetuals. Interest on some perpetuals is contingent on dividends on equity. *Always read the small print in the prospectus.*
Zero-coupon bonds	Corporations/banks/building societies/governments/ government agencies	No coupon payments. Interest payments are received at maturity. Usually issued at a discount and redeemed at par.

| Medium-term notes | Corporations/banks/ governments/government agencies | Pay fixed coupon. Issued on 'tap' basis. Because issuing procedure is similar to CDs and rotation can be as short as one year, this product falls into both money and bond market categories. |

---

4. DERIVATIVE MARKET*

Main instruments	**Usual issuers**	**Special features**
Forwards/futures/ options/warrants	Banks/corporations	Traded OTC or on exchanges. Prices move in relation to underlying asset/ instrument. Limited life.

A derivative product cannot exist without an underlying product.

Caution: *Subordinated debt has a lower repayment ranking. In particular, perpetual FRNs are more like equity than other bonds, in this respect. To reiterate, always read the small print in the prospectus.*

For a product to be actively traded and afforded the full-time attention of a trader, there needs to be sufficient supply and turnover in it and thus opportunities to make money.

Borrowers and investors

Borrowers and investors fall into the groups set out below.

Typical borrowers	**Typical investors**
• Banks, including central banks	• Banks, including central banks
• Building societies	• Building societies
• Corporations	• Charitable trusts
• Governments and their agencies	• Corporations
• Municipalities	• Fund managers
• Supranational entities	• Governments and their agencies/municipalities
• Utilities	• Individuals
	• Insurance companies
	• Local authorities
	• Pension funds
	• Supranational entities (IMF, World Bank, etc.)
	• Unions

'Borrowed' funds can be used in various ways. For example, a government may use borrowings to finance a trade deficit, pay interest charges and/or redeem, existing debt, pay for defence expenditure/space projects, buy other currencies in the foreign exchange markets in order to support their own currency, finance contributions/donations to other countries, pay for exploration and extraction of natural resources such as oil. Local authorities/municipalities may borrow money to develop/improve infrastructure (roads, rail-tracks, bridges, airports, sanitation, utilities etc.). A corporation may borrow money to pay for acquisitions of other companies, or for product development and expansion; to pay for new premises, plant and equipment, or for research and development in order to maintain their competitive edge. A bank or building society may borrow money to on-lend to customers, while supranational entities such as the IBRD and the EBRD, borrow to on-lend to developing countries.

Inside a major house - key departments and responsibilities

The following are the key departments you will find within a typical house, if it is a major player in the markets, together with a brief description of each department's duties and responsibilities.

■ Secondary Trading Department
Buys and sells securities that are no longer 'new issues'. This can be done for a firm's own account and/or on behalf of investors, the aim being to make as much money as possible!

■ Sales Department
Responsible for building good relationships with investors and providing them with investment advice, so as to transact profitable business by buying and selling securities.

■ Syndicate Department
Handles all primary market activities. Decides the terms and conditions for all new issues when acting as lead manager, and assesses invitations to participate in a lesser capacity in deals lead-managed by competitors. Also responsible for syndicating (e.g. distributing) participations in new issues. Note that while the majority of syndicate managers bear ultimate responsibility for both the pricing and syndication of new deals, some only handle the syndication process. In these cases, the pricing of a new deal is arrived at by internal consensus through discussion with the secondary trading staff.

■ Finance Department
Responsible for obtaining money to support syndicate and trading activities, i.e. to finance inventories. As the liquidity requirements of a major house will invariably exceed their capital, they will need to borrow money in various currencies on an ongoing basis. A finance department may also handle the borrowing and lending of securities via the repo market, and actively trade the repo market for profit.

■ Financial Engineering/Structured Product Department
Responsible for creating products with structures that satisfy the needs of both borrowers and investors. Also re-structures existing instruments so as to increase their appeal with investors, if money can be made or saved by doing so.

■ Investment Banking Department
Responsible for building good relationships with entities in need of money, the aim being to either provide advice in return for fee income, or to secure, ideally profitable, mandates for new issues.

■ Corporate Finance/Mergers & Acquisitions Department
Provides general advice on how to raise money, and advises on mergers and acquisitions (M&A) between companies, in return for fee income.

■ Research Department
- *Credit Research:* Analyses countries, industries and individual companies to assess their short and long term creditworthiness, and in turn their ability to repay their debts.
- *Product Research:* Analyses specific markets and financial products.
- *Economic Research:* Analyses the flows of money around the world and the economies of all major nations, with the aim of accurately predicting both short- and long-term interest rate movements.

The collective input from the various research departments, helps a firm to protect its own capital and to advise its clients better.

■ Compliance Department
Ensures compliance with all regulatory/legal requirements.

■ Operations Department
Operations house a host of crucial functions including: the clearance and settlement of all transactions, telecommunications, and technological and systems support (see Chapters 7 and 12).

Here I have concentrated on areas relevant to this book, although there are many others that are crucial to the smooth running of an organization, such as accounting and human resources.

Chapter 4

GLOSSARY FOR CHAPTER 4

basis point (bp)
1/100th of one per cent. Commonly used in the business in both terms of price and yield.

bid
Buying price. The price at which a trader will buy

bond switch
The sale of one bond and the purchase of another, usually for an increase in yield or improvement in credit quality or structure.

CMO
Collateralized mortgage obligation, i.e. a debt instrument that is backed by a pool of mortgages which are the source of all interest payments and principal on the debt security.

execution
Completion of a transaction, i.e. if a client places an order to buy a specific amount of a specific security, when the trader completes the order he will have 'executed' the trade and the salesperson will call the client to report an 'execution'.

face value
The amount written on the face of a bond certificate, i.e. the nominal amount to be repaid at maturity. *See also* **par value** in the Glossary for Chapter 3.

fixed
Fixed-rate securities, where the rate of interest payable to holders is fixed for the life of the instrument. i.e. a bond with a 10 per cent annual coupon will pay interest at the rate of 10 per cent of face value for each year the bond is outstanding.

FRN
Floating-rate note, so called because the rate of interest payable to holders is adjusted periodically in relation to a benchmark such as Libor.

hit
Term used to describe a (sometimes unwanted) purchase of bonds, i.e. "I've just been hit at 99".

mm
Abbreviation for million.

offer
Offering price. The price at which a trader will sell.

partials
An abbreviation for 'partial execution', i.e. whether a client will be happy to just buy two million bonds when their preference is to buy five million, or is their order/interest on an 'all or none' basis.

position securities
The buying and short-selling of securities is known as the *positioning* of securities. Securities owned are known as *long* positions while securities sold, but not owned, are known as *short* positions.

portfolio
Securities owned by an individual or institution for investment purposes.

subject
Short for *subject to confirmation,* indicating a potential—but not firm—proposal.

trader
A person who buys and sells (trades) securities; also called a *dealer* or *market-maker* and sometimes a *broker. See* Glossary for Chapter 5.

unlisted
Securities, i.e. notes/bonds that are not listed on a designated exchange such as the London Stock Exchange or the Luxembourg Stock Exchange.

write tickets
Street-speak for doing business. A salesperson who writes a lot of tickets is one who does a lot of business.

Chapter 4

Sales

Enjoyment is the key to achieving maximum effect in a job. Selling securities is hard work. It takes skill and judgement and consistent effort. Whilst the aim is to transact profitable business, it is critical that results are achieved without any dilution in company image or personal credibility. To ensure both your own and employer's long-term success, your sales approach must be rooted in integrity and a sincere desire to provide a good service.

First, understand the house for which you work and be clear about what makes a 'good' client so you know what you are trying to achieve. Most important of all, know your customers well and understand their investment criteria and objectives thoroughly. Know your key competitors' strengths and weaknesses, and work out how to differentiate yourself and your firm, in a meaningful way.

Understanding your employer

It is essential to know your employer's general philosophy, their short- and long-term aims, and in particular what is expected of you, and within what time frame. Your efforts could otherwise be misdirected and undervalued. You also need to know your firm's strengths and weaknesses and how to make the most of its resources. Moreover, cultivate good relationships with your traders and understand their needs and expectations. (*See* Chapter 8, 'Sales-trading relationships').

Understanding your objective

Clients *per se* are ten a penny. Good clients are rare, and the result of much effort. As a salesperson your job is to cultivate relationships and build a client base that pays its way. To this end, earn your clients' trust and respect. Once achieved, be sure never to abuse it. The securities business is incestuous. People gossip and competition is fierce. By exploiting a client's trust, you will hurt yourself and your employer. There are no lasting short cuts. In pursuit of building a good client base you must provide:

- Consistent coverage of the account;
- Professional back-up coverage in your absence;
- Competitive prices;
- Liquidity;
- Original ideas;
- Efficient clearance of transactions;
- Swift handling of any clearance problem;
- Obvious integrity.

Over time, you should expect your clients, in return, to:

- Call you first when they are looking to trade;
- Disclose whether they want to buy or sell;
- Leave you an order if you so require it;
- Not penny-pinch to the last fraction of a basis point, particularly when executing trade ideas that you suggest, and which they would not otherwise have known about.

Last but not least, a good—indeed a highly-valuable—client, is one who does the majority of his or her business with you, and who is willing to pay for good investment advice. When measuring your effectiveness as a salesperson therefore, compare how much of your clients' business you are capturing *vis-à-vis* your competitors, and assess your performance as compared with colleagues. A highly-effective salesperson, is one who not only has good clients, but also manages to capture the majority of each client's business.

Knowing your customer

Rule Number One in sales is to know each of your clients well. There is a lot involved. For example, the nature of a client's business, the source of their funds and the cost of those funds, as well as their investment criteria and objectives, and what type of service they require. Once this information is in place, you are then in a position to devise an appropriately focused and time-efficient sales strategy for servicing the account. You must then work on building a rapport with each person with whom you speak on a regular basis.

With effort, it is always possible to find common ground with a client. Whatever a client's interests—antiques, art, astrology, children (making children!), food, sport, wine, whatever—learn something about the subject. You will be surprised how an initial forced interest in something can turn into a genuine appreciation.

As a salesperson learn to read your clients' moods and temperaments, and when and when not to overstep the mark. A touch of over-familiarity at the wrong time, especially early on, can kill the relationship. Be respectful of clients' feelings and sensitive to how they perceive both you and your firm. Remember, you are dealing with another human being, and should therefore approach any situation in a sincere and sensible way.

The following is a list of useful and essential information you will need to know about each of your clients in order to provide them with a good service:

- Core business activity;
- Major shareholders/owners;
- Accounting year end;
- Number of portfolio managers and whether they are specialists or generalists;
- The names of all individuals with authority to make trading decisions;
- Whether, and if so how often, investment meetings are held to decide strategy;
- The approval procedure for investments in new currencies, credits and structures, and how long this takes;
- Whether the institution has a separate trading division and if so, whether transactions have to be passed to that division for execution;
- If a trading division (dealing arm) exists, will anyone in that division ever get to know about business transacted with you;
- The name(s) of settlements staff who handle settlement problems/queries;
- Whether the client receives any research material or market information from any division of your firm;
- Currency(ies) in which funds are denominated, and the cost of those funds;
- Which currencies the client can invest in (e.g. Canadian dollars, Italian lira, sterling, US dollars, Japanese yen, etc.);
- Which products the client can invest in (e.g. MTNs, FRNs, eurobonds, CMOs, government securities, derivative instruments, etc.);
- The maturity constraints for each product;
- Size of portfolio, mix between debt and equity, and details of current holdings;
- The:
    a) average size of each holding;
    b) minimum investment grade for bond issues;
    c) minimum yield pick-up and/or cash take-out required on bond switches;
    d) percentage of any one issue the client can own;
    e) percentage of any one name the client can own;

- Whether there are any special taxation treaties/loopholes that the client can take advantage of through investment in certain products and/or countries;
- The relative importance of capital gain and current income;
- The measurements used to assess the performance of the portfolio(s);
- Whether the client can:
  a) take losses;
  b) buy securities above face value;
  c) buy new issues;
  d) buy unlisted securities;
  e) invest in derivative instruments and, if so, which ones.

This list is not in any particular order, and nor is it exhaustive but, as one salesperson can be responsible for servicing as many as forty clients, it provides an insight into what is involved in selling securities. All of this information needs to be stored for future reference, either on computer or on hard copy. Many salespeople keep their own records in a style that suits them. However, with this approach it can be hard for back-up staff to read and understand a salesperson's notes in his/her absence. For this reason I think it is more efficient to use a standard format.

Figure 4.1 shows my preferred layout for storing investment parameter information. Although the layout has been reduced in size to fit the pages of this book, enlarging it to A4 will provide a comfortably-sized document, enabling you both to enter and retrieve information in a quick and easy manner. You will, however, need to use abbreviations. For example, if a client cannot—or will not—buy eurobonds longer than seven years, I would write 'OT 7 yrs' rather than 'out to 7 years' in the 'euros' column

A client's thought process

The mental process investors go through when deciding whether to buy, sell or hold, is often not that different from that of traders. Chapter 6, on the thought process of dealers, could therefore help clarify the way clients think. While there maybe differences—due to time horizon, risk profile, etc.—their quest to make money is the same. When reading this chapter, bear in mind that the questions that dealers ask themselves about their competitors, are not dissimilar to those that your clients will be asking about you!

Getting along with your traders

Regard your traders as clients. To be effective as a salesperson you need their support. If you do not get along with a trader, he or she is unlikely to show you their best idea first, or put their best foot forward when quoting

Client name	Core business

| Does client have its own trading desk? - Yes/No. If 'Yes', are the traders ever likely to know about business transacted with you? - Yes/ No ||

Size of portfolio	Currencies in which funds are denominated and the average cost of those funds

Below, you can simply circle that which applies

Needs Current Income / Capital Gain	Liquidity: Vital / Important / Depends
Can/Cannot take losses	Can/Cannot pay premium
Can/Cannot but new issues	Can/Cannot buy unlisted securities
Can/Cannot do asset swaps and structured transactions	Can/Cannot trade futures/options

| Can/Cannot do hedged currency trades ||

| Minimum criteria and yield pick-up for bond switches ||

| Minimum investment grade required ||

| Names of people with authority to make trading decisions ||

| New names/structures approved by:
 How long does the approval process take? ||

CAN BUY THE FOLLOWING PRODUCTS (* Indicates tax advantage)

	CAD	DEM	NLG	XEU	FRF	GBP	USD	JPY
Governments								
Other domestic products								
Euros								
FRNs								
Money market products								
Equity								
Warrants								
Convertibles								
Other								

Figure 4.1   Sample layout for storing investment parameter information

prices to your clients. The reality is that if you do not get along with your traders, it will be a lot harder to write tickets. This is human nature. It is essential therefore, to cultivate good relations with them. Chapters 6 and 8 look at what both traders and salespeople can do to help each other in their daily work.

Knowing your competitors

It is critical to know the strengths and weaknesses of your main competitors, and how your firm compares. Each of your clients will deal with a few firms most of the time. Consult league tables to find out which houses are active in which markets, and ask friends in the business, and colleagues, for their input. Once mutual trust and respect is established, it should also be possible to find out from your clients which houses they deal with and what they most value about each firm, as well as the salesperson who services them. Be aware, too, that certain companies specialize in conducting surveys among investors about the quality of products and services provided by the Street. These findings can be purchased.

Constantly ask questions in order to know what your competitors are doing, and the degree of success they are achieving with your clients. A competitive analysis is a prerequisite to developing an effective sales strategy.

Making a difference

You can make a positive difference in a number of simple ways. Filtering research for example, rather than deluging customers with every item of information your firm generates, could set you apart as someone who understands relevances and who appreciates how precious little time your clients have.

Preparing sales calls well, and providing all necessary details on a proposed transaction at the outset, will save customers having to ask questions, and will attest to your respect for them. This, too, can make a difference in your favour. It may seem like common sense to provide all relevant information in the first instance, but salespeople have been known, in their haste to write a ticket, to call a client with half a story. While you may be convinced that an idea is brilliant, your client will need to be taken through the merits of the transaction, and provided with all the relevant details on each security in question. If your client does not have sufficient information to make a decision, you risk the market moving away, the opportunity disappearing, and your client being frustrated at having devoted the time to listening to you in the first place.

When working out how to make your sales approach different, think of ways that can also save time. Writing a daily or weekly report that is three pages long may seem like a good idea, but doing so would draw on your time and that of your clients. A one-page concise rundown on a market, prepared on a standardized form that makes it easy for clients to scan, could be both useful and keep you on your toes. Just remember to keep things short and simple.

Focus

There is an old saying 'Do not confuse motion with action'. Misguided or unfocused action leads to not very much at all. There are plenty of people out there who are busy, busy, busy, going nowhere fast. The key to getting things done is to be focused. As a salesperson, your job is to focus on clients with whom you can do good business, and then, on a daily basis, the priorities of both your traders and clients.

In general, the better the relationship with a client, the more business you can do with them. This is only true, however, if you focus on clients whose structure and investment parameters enable good quality business. It is not in your own or your employer's interests to devote a lot of time to a client with whom you cannot do good business, whatever the reasons. Remember that it is also better to focus on getting business done in products in which your firm has a credible presence. You will risk losing credibility and the relationship, by trying to capture business in markets in which you cannot be competitive.

Focus on trades which are good for both clients and traders, and which you have a good chance of achieving. Win-win situations do exist. If your trader makes a profit, it does not mean your client sustains a loss, as reinvestment in other securities could ultimately provide a better return. Differing opinions and perceptions are what make a market.

Key traits

As a salesperson, it is essential to know what and what not to say, how and how not to say it, when and when not to say it, and if you decide to say it at all, to whom to say it! Understand the precise needs of both traders and clients, and use words and actions that endear yourself to (or at least do not alienate yourself from) both parties. Good communication skills are therefore essential. You must listen, and learn how to communicate in a constructive and diplomatic way. Be honest, focused, organized, willing to work hard and imaginative.

At the start of each day, you will have a degree of freedom of choice in terms of what products/markets to get involved in. Look for new ways to communicate the appeal of an investment or disinvestment. Do not try to be gimmicky, instead concentrate on uncovering historical facts and combining them with your predictions for the future, to produce a logical and convincing argument. If you cannot, maybe the idea is not that good.

Instead of focusing on why something does not work, focus on how to get it to work. A simple example would be to run price histories between two or more securities and/or markets to see if anything is historically out of line. Do remember though, that the past need not necessarily be a precedent.

You just have to know more than the rest (and certainly as much, if not more than your clients!), and work harder than everyone else.

Organization

Time is money. You will not be the only salesperson ringing a client with an idea. An opportunity can disappear in minutes—timing is critical. It is thus essential to be organized and have systems in place that enable you to identify which of your clients could be interested in a particular trade, within minutes of an opportunity arising. IP (investment parameter) sheets have been designed with this in mind. And remember, time is not just money in terms of how much you are paid: a missed opportunity, due to inefficiency, can cost many thousands of dollars in lost revenue.

Preparing your sales call

Compiling, on a standardized sheet, all necessary information on securities you are looking to buy and/or sell, before calling clients is essential. It can save time and better ensure that you have all relevant details to assess the merits of a trade before making a call. Chapter 8, 'Sales-trading relationships', contains a standardized format for presenting trade ideas. This can also be used to prepare sales calls.

Keeping track of trades and potential trades

I would also recommend creating a standardized form into which you can log details of every trade done, and with whom, on any given day. This will facilitate a speedy response in the event of a trade discrepancy. Customers often want to trade at prices that differ considerably from current market levels. Since markets change all the time, prices that appear unrealistic one day can turn out to be very achievable the next. 'TR' (trade reminder) slips detailing the prices at which a client will do a particular trade, help to ensure opportunities are not missed. Most houses have their own version of TR slips, usually with three or four carbon copies in different colours, enabling all individuals involved to have a copy. A trade reminder slip should contain the information shown in Figure 4.2.

Date: **Name of salesperson:**

Subject, *(client name or code)* **would like to:**

Buy/Sell	Amount	Issuer of security	CPN	Maturity	Price	Yield
Buy	$5mm	Sweden	8½	6/15/98	100	8.50
Sell	$5mm	Denmark	8½	6/15/98	100	8.50

Comments:

Will do partials. This trade is a reversal of a previous trade, etc.

Figure 4.2   A sample trade reminder slip

General sales tips

- Before calling a client for the first time, check the institution's historical relationship with your firm in case the client has suffered from inconsistent and/or poor coverage in the past. Always remember to ask if it is a good time to talk. Thereafter, and to encourage dialogue, ask a few 'open' questions: questions which cannot be answered with a straight yes or no. In addition:
- Make absolutely sure that you have correct settlement instructions before doing a trade.
- Prepare your story well. Compile all the details on a security before picking up the telephone. Check proposed trades against 'IP' sheets to ensure that the trade you intend to propose does indeed make sense for your client.
- Be thorough and speedy when dealing with settlement problems.
- Work with your trader to supply more than just a market, when a client asks for a two-way price (both a bid and an offer). Speculate on what the client is trying to achieve and try to come up with an intelligent alternative. This will show that you care, which will inspire confidence and help build greater trust.
- Inform your client *immediately* if your company's view on a security you have sold them, changes for the worse. Do this even if your client loses money by liquidating the position.

- Avoid taking orders if there is less than a 50/50 chance of execution. When taking orders, always let the customer know what the odds of execution are. Taking orders when it is unlikely that your firm can do the trade, can damage your own, as well as your employer's, image.
- Remember that people change their minds all the time. Any client's level of interest in an idea will depend on their priorities at the time of your call. People change their minds all the time. The way you feel today about a certain matter could be very different to the way you felt last week; clients are people. Do not, therefore, make up your clients minds for them. If your trader suggests an idea for a particular client, unless you are 100 per cent sure that the client will not do the trade, always show them the idea. Always ask the question if you are in any doubt, and do not be afraid to re-present an idea that a client rejects for no good reason the first time it is shown to them.

Measuring your performance

IP (investment parameter) sheets can help identify which clients are paying their way. This in turn can help you and your superiors assess your performance.

It is difficult to know whether a set of volume figures is good, bad or indifferent unless there is a relative measure of one client versus another, as well as some idea of what percentage of overall business any volume numbers represent. It could help therefore, to create production targets based on the size of a client's portfolio and expected activity levels. This would enable you to see where your time is best spent. Your sales manager(s) could then see whether you were doing a better job than your colleagues, relatively speaking.

Some sales managers, when carrying out account reviews, will re-assign an account to another salesperson if they are dissatisfied with the amount of business being done. IP sheets that contain facts, can help reduce speculation and assumption, and aid your appraisal.

Precise communication

Always, always, always repeat back every detail of a trade at the time of execution to your trader first, and then to your client. Never confirm a trade with a client until confirmed with your trader. Be sure to speak to the client from your firm's point of view. If the client is buying, your firm is selling, and you should confirm using the words 'We sell to you'. It is essential to get the terms 'bid' and 'offer' straight in your mind. If your trader is bidding for a security, your job is to find a seller who will either hit your trader's bid, or make a counter-offer.

When a client asks for a bid, it means they would like to sell, in which case you should ask the trader for his bid, being the price at which he will buy from the client. If on the other hand, a client gives you a bid, then they would like to buy, and you should ask the trader for an offer, being the price at which he will sell to the client! It can be confusing, which is why it is absolutely vital that you adopt a method of communication that is clear and precise, and not open to misinterpretation by either traders or clients.

General communication

Open questions can be invaluable in building and strengthening relationships, and/or extracting information, since they cannot be answered with a simple 'Yes' or 'No'. Thus communication barriers can be more easily dissolved, which can be particularly useful when dealing with a new client or a colleague with whom you find it hard to communicate.

Open questions begin with 'What?', 'When?', 'Why?', 'Where?' or 'How?' and they force the other person to communicate more with you.

For example, if you want to find out what is going on in another department or market, it is no use asking if there is anything going on. You need to ask What is going on? Where is it all happening? How did it all come about? Who was involved? and Why did it happen? etc. Open questions can help to:

- Open up a broader picture: 'What do you think makes (a firm or individual) so successful?'
- Obtain concrete information: 'What particular aspect of the structure concerns you?' 'When is the best time for me call you?' 'How can we be most useful to you?'
- Explore facts and feelings: 'What caused you to trade away?' 'Where did I go wrong?' 'What could I have done differently?' 'How would you have liked me to have handled the situation?'
- Obtain specific explanations 'Why do you prefer XYZ?'

However, open questions yield little if they are abrupt or accusatory:

'Why the....didn't you tell me he was a seller?' 'Why did you do that?' 'What the....are you doing over there?' 'Where on earth have you been?' 'How in God's name did that happen?'

Open questions expressed in this way are best avoided.

Chapter 5

GLOSSARY FOR CHAPTER 5

broker, broke (to)
A firm that intermediates between buyers and sellers but does not use its own capital to take positions is called a *broker*. Although dealers are sometimes called brokers, technically speaking *to broke* securities is to buy from one party and sell to another simultaneously for a small profit (a brokerage fee, also called a *turn*), without taking any market risk.

liquidate
To liquidate is to buy or sell a security to extinguish a position.

Registered Dealers
Houses that are registered as market-makers in a security with the Council of Reporting Dealers (CRD) a semi-autonomous arm of ISMA. Registered market makers are listed in ISMA's directory, which is used by market professionals and investors to ascertain which firm to call for a price.

retail customers
Investors. *See* Glossary for Chapter 1.

Chapter 5

What makes a 'good' client?

The term *client* is a loose one and is used to describe any institution serviced by a salesperson. However, some of these institutions operate more like brokers, buying from one house and selling to another simultaneously, for a small profit, without taking any market risk. As a salesperson, it is in your own, as well as your firm's, interests to devote time and energy to servicing clients with whom you can do the best quality business. You therefore need some criteria to determine the quality of clients, and the type and level of service they should receive. Notwithstanding the fact that every house will want access to all of the flows (flows of business being done), your time is valuable and is best spent servicing genuine investors who can and want to do business.

One relatively simple and quick approach, is to separate clients into three categories based on: their source of funds, how long they can own securities, and their involvement in competing activities. It is also worth assessing the manner in which clients conduct themselves in the market-place. If unhappy with their approach, explain how your firm would like to operate and why. Your clients assess the way you and your firm conduct business, and there is no reason why you should not do the same.

Grade One clients

The qualifying criteria for Grade One clients, which I consider the best type, is as follows:

- A natural flow of funds used to finance investments;
- Capacity to own securities for long periods, though able to actively trade their portfolio to increase return;
- No market-making activities, or if they do exist, no pressure on portfolio managers to deal with their market-making arms.[1]

---

[1] *If a portfolio manager is required to pass trade ideas to his trading division for execution, you may not wish to make him your first call with a new money-making opportunity. It is all a matter of what possible outlets exist at any point in time for any particular trade.*

I would also place *spread bankers* in Grade One. These are banks that obtain funds (such as short-term eurodollars) which can be used to invest in complementary assets (such as FRNs), but where such investments can be held for the longer term if necessary.

It is important to know what genuine Grade One investors are doing, since they represent the deepest source of liquidity. Moreover, you can make more money covering these type of accounts, and have future access to the securities you sell to them. Last but not least, there is always a price that works. Even if a swap is necessary, providing the structure and creditworthiness is acceptable and the client is not full on the name (some clients limit the amount they invest in any one name to a percentage of all outstanding debt), a price can always be established.

The only disadvantage of dealing with Grade One investors is that they sometimes take time responding.

Please note, that here we are looking at investors in the bond markets. Investors in short-term assets do not, generally-speaking, fall into this category. Corporations investing surplus operating cash for short periods of time are genuine investors, and thus when grading such accounts, bear in mind the limitations/restrictions that arise as a result of the nature of a client's business.

Grade Two clients

Grade Two clients differ from Grade One in that they do not have a natural flow of funds, such as insurance premiums or pension contributions. Their sole reason for existence is to make money trading the markets, using both their own capital, as well as wholesale funds, over a relatively short time frame. These clients are generally known as *arbitrageurs* because they specialize in 'anomaly' trading.

Although their interest in owning securities for a long time may be limited, many Grade Two clients have the capacity to trade in very big amounts and can therefore be a valuable source of liquidity. You need to be quite experienced and sophisticated to cover these type of clients, as their proximity to the Street means they will often know as much—if not more—than you and your traders about what is going on. This type of client usually comprises extremely smart, analytically-minded individuals who know their way around the Street very well. If you are a basis point off market in your price, a Grade Two client is likely to deal with you—like it or not!

Grade Three clients

Grade Three clients differ from the above in that they are not generally the end-investor, but linked, via a franchise, with certain customers that could be hard to access directly. They may borrow funds from the wholesale market and position securities, e.g. trade for their own account, much like full-blown securities firms. They may also have a group of salespeople servicing some of the same clients as yourself.

While Grade Three clients may choose to quote two-way prices to their customers, they do not usually quote prices to other dealers, as they are seldom listed as reporting dealers. They may also have market-making activities in certain products. While some evolve to become professional houses, many prefer their double status: *professional* when calling customers, and *client* when calling the Street. Personally, I feel that such clients should be serviced by a 'dealer contact' desk and treated like professionals, so that professional dealers at major houses have the option of quoting a price, but are not obliged to do so.

Whilst it is useful for a firm to have access to these sort of clients in order to be aware of the flows of business occurring, I do not feel they deserve to be covered by an experienced salesperson. As a salesperson you should not show your best ideas to them, as you may find they then call one of your other clients with the idea before you do.

Many, many, arguments occur between traders and salespeople because of Grade Three clients. For example, if your trader owns ten million bonds, and you sell five million to a Grade Three client who then sells them to one or more professional houses for a few cents profit, your trader will naturally be furious. The price could go down and reduce his chances of selling the balance of the bonds. Also, your trader could have done this without your so-called help. Finally, because you have not sold the bonds to a genuine end-investor, you do not know where to find them at a later date.

If a Grade Three client has a franchise in a geographic region where your firm is weak, you may be able to do some good business. Do be aware however, of the potential overlap.

Summary

Some traders regard client business as a waste of time, and do the majority of their business with other professionals. I think such a view stems largely from traders being used as a pricing service by Grade Three clients. When dealing with genuine investors, such as Grade One and Grade Two clients, there are numerous advantages, the key ones of which are:

- access to the real flows
- greater profit potential
- future access to securities
- access to the deepest source of liquidity
- there is always a price that works

While the Street can sometimes facilitate speedier liquidation, essential when a trader's interest-rate view changes, the trader will not know where to find the securities at a later date. The profit margin is also less and, most critical of all, without knowing what genuine investors are doing, a trader can end up with a highly distorted perception of what is happening. Genuine investor flow is what ultimately drives and supports any market. Chapter 21, 'Avoiding disasters' illustrates what can go wrong if you trade without direct access to investors.

A competitor is not a substitute for a client. A professional house should be regarded as no more than an avenue via which a trader can:

- liquidate unattractive securities
- acquire attractive securities
- liquidate quickly

In order to provide the best service to clients and achieve the best results from them, traders and salespeople have to work very closely together.

Chapter 6

GLOSSARY FOR CHAPTER 6

as principal
When a firm uses its own capital, it is acting as principal.

bearish
Pessimistic on the market, expecting prices to go lower.

bullish
Optimistic on the market, expecting prices to go higher.

benchmark
A base upon which the yield or price of a security is determined. For example, an FRN may pay interest at the rate of 6-month Libor + 20bp and a new issue may be priced to offer a yield above or below US government securities, in which case Libor and US government bonds would represent benchmarks.

colour
Another term for information. To give colour on a market is to provide information about what is going on.

commodity
A natural resource such as food produce or precious metals/stones.

face amount
See **par value** in the Glossary for Chapter 3.

feel
Term to describe a dealer's opinion and expectations for his market. Also called *intuition*.

hedge
A trade entered into for the express purpose of protecting existing positions against adverse market movements.

indication
An indication is an approximate idea of where a security is trading, not a firm price at which one can trade.

issuer(s)
Borrower(s). Entities that raise money in the markets by 'issuing' securities such as shares or bonds.

key issue(s)

The most recently-issued government bonds in the US domestic market. These are often used as benchmarks for assessing value on other similarly-structured securities.

lifted/taken/lost

Terms used to describe a sale of bonds. If a dealer says 'I've just been lifted', he means he has just made a price (a market) and that his counterparty (which could be a competitor or a client) has dealt on his offering price and has purchased securities from him.

to make a market

To provide both a bid price and an offer price in a security. If a dealer, when asked for a market, responds '99 bid', he is only providing a one-way market. A market usually comprises a two-way price, i.e. both a 'bid' and an 'offer'.

market

The eurobond market and the stock market are umbrella terms under which fall the trading of a variety of securities. If you ask a dealer in US dollar-denominated eurobonds, 'What's the market doing?', your question would relate to the major bond market influencing the US$ eurobond market, which would be the US government bond market. If you asked, 'What's your market doing?' then the enquiry would relate to the dollar eurobond market and, more specifically, the particular sector of the market he trades.

P+L

Profit and loss.

plain vanilla

A bond with a conventional structure, usually taken to mean a fixed-rate security with a common maturity, i.e. between 5-10 years.

point

One percentage point which is equal to 100 basis points (bp), used in the context of both prices and yields.

position

long position: To own securities. If a dealer says "I'm long the market", he means that he owns securities, which should mean that he expects prices to go higher.

short position: When a dealer is 'short the market', it means he has sold securities that he does not own, and which he will have to buy back (cover) at some point. Except for hedging purposes, if a short position is established deliberately in a particular security then the dealer would be expecting the price of that security to fall.

flat position: When a dealer is neither long nor short the market on a net basis. For example, if a dealer owns (is 'long') 50,000,000 bonds and is also short 50,000,000 other bonds he would have a net flat position. A position of 50 million long and 30 million short would equal a net long position of 20 million. To be completely flat is to be neither long nor short in any security.

rally
A rise in prices due to increased demand. This can occur for a variety of reasons such as a revaluation as a result of a positive change in economic fundamentals, a market turnaround following a period of consistent selling, an imbalance in supply and demand etc.

ramp
When a dealer buys lots of a security and forces up the price to a level where it has no value relative to other comparable bonds.

rating agency
A company that grades, or *rates*, borrowers and/or specific bonds. A rating helps investors assess an issuer's financial health and ability to honour their debt obligations. An 'AAA' (or, a 'Triple-A') rating means one can be confident that an issuer can meet all interest payments and principal repayment at maturity. However, sometimes an AAA rating is assigned to a specific issue because it is collateralized with top quality assets from where all interest and principal comes. Standard & Poor's, Moody's and Duff & Phelps are three of the bigger rating agencies. A borrower that is assigned an AAA rating is in excellent financial health, whereas one that is assigned a CCC rating is more risky and may not, for example, be in business when its debt obligations mature. Ratings can and do change.

relative value
The appeal of one bond or market relative to another, i.e. to compare one bond against another similar bond to assess its attractiveness. For two bonds to be compared, they need to be of similar credit standing and structure.

spread
The yield differential between a benchmark (such as Libor) and a security (*see* **yield curve**, below), or between two different securities or markets. For example, if the yield between five-year bonds issued by Ford and General Motors had been consistent at, say, 50bp but then widened to 100bp dealers would say that 'the spread had widened'.

subject
Not firm, indicating a need to check before confirming.

squeezed
When unusually large amounts of a security are purchased in an attempt to control the price, then the security is referred to as being squeezed.

swap/switch
The sale and purchase of two securities. *See* **bond switch** in the Glossary for Chapter 4.

yield
An abbreviation for *yield-to-maturity*, which is the rate of return on a security based on its coupon, maturity and price.

yield curve
A graphical illustration of yield levels for a particular market.

inverted curve: An inverted curve means that long term interest rates are lower than short term interest rates.

off the curve: When a security is trading 'off the curve' it means it is cheaper (higher yielding) than benchmark government bonds.

positive curve: A positive curve means that long-term interest rates are higher than short-term interest rates.

through the curve: When a security is trading 'through the curve' it means it is more expensive (offering a lower yield) than benchmark government bonds.

Chapter 6

Trading

The focus of this chapter is the trading of international securities with maturities longer than one year. The trading principles can, however, be applied to the money, bond and equity markets, or indeed any market in any commodity. I know this to be the case, as I began my career as a street trader in the true sense of the word. I sold fruit, vegetables, ice cream, shellfish and a variety of other perishable produce throughout my childhood and, thereafter, traded a variety of bonds for Salomon Brothers. To illustrate my point, I will start with an analogy to car dealing. The considerations of a car dealer are as extensive as those of a bond dealer, and thus provide a good parallel for would-be bond dealers.

Trading cars

John, a car dealer, asks you, another car dealer, to bid on a fleet of 20 new BMWs—with a current book price of $50,000 each. What will be your bid, i.e. what price should you pay? What questions do you need answers to, in order to work out the price at which you would be happy to buy these cars?

- Where will you go if you have to buy the cars? Where can you sell them?
- How long will it take you to sell them?
- How much will it cost you to finance them? If you have to borrow money to do so, will you incur interest charges? Even if you are investing your own cash, you must look at what alternative assets you could buy that would provide you with a greater return.
- What additional costs are you likely to incur if you end up buying these cars? e.g. tax, insurance, future transportation to buyers, etc.
- Will settlements be easy to effect? Are these vehicles available for quick delivery, or is John part of a chain?
- What do you think your competitors will pay? Are they long, short or flat in the BMW sector, and the car sector in general?
- Will it be easy for you to sell these cars? Will potential buyers know enough about this model or will you have to produce some marketing material to promote them?
- How easy is it to maintain BMWs? Are parts easy to obtain and are there enough service stations around the country?

- Will maintenance costs encourage or deter potential buyers?
- Is it likely that John has already shown this business away, i.e. approached other dealers and/or clients before coming to you?
- Is it possible that John will let you buy just a few cars and work on an order to sell the balance (e.g. could you have some on 'sale or return').
- What are BMW doing? Are they about to launch a replacement model?
- What are other car manufacturers doing? Are Ford, Chrysler, Rolls-Royce, Mercedes, etc., about to release a new competing car on to the market that could be more appealing than the BMWs you are going to bid on, and could therefore end up owning?
- What is happening to the oil price? Any rise in the oil price will increase the price of petrol/gasoline.
- Do your potential customers have surplus cash that they could use to buy new BMWs, or would they have to borrow money to do so? If they had to borrow funds, how much will it cost them? (e.g. what are short-term interest rates/current credit terms?).
- How would you redistribute these cars? Would you have to commit lots of your time, and the time of your salespeople, in order to sell them? Could this time be better spent? (e.g. does the potential profit justify the resources required to successfully liquidate this position?)

Deciding to buy all 20 cars at the current book price of $50,000 each, would mean a bid of $1,000,000, but you would need to be sure that the cars could be distributed at something more than book price, in order to make a profit.

It may even make sense to bid more than book value. For example, if from your investigations you concluded that supply was tight, and demand for these cars was very high, you might decide to bid more than book price, and then commit a little more money to buying any surplus supplies that may be in the hands of other car dealers, so as to gain control of the market. You could then re-offer all the cars at a new higher level of, say, $60,000 each. The market however, would need to be convinced that the cars still represented good value at $60,000, as compared to alternative models available.

The obligations and functions of a bond trader

A bond trader's chief responsibility is to make money without compromising their employer's image in any way. To this end, they take positions, that is, buy and sell securities using their employer's capital. Some traders are also market-makers, and are therefore obliged to provide bids and offers to both competitors and clients upon request.

The previous analogy looked quite simply, at putting on a bid without obligation, i.e. you were not forced to bid. A trader however, in the issues in which his firm is registered as a reporting dealer with the Council of

Reporting Dealers (CRD - a semi-autonomous arm of ISMA) is required to bid and to provide an offer as well! Failure to do so can result in sanctions.

What would you do for example, if John had asked you for a two-way price, i.e. both a bid and offer—a price at which you would buy 20 cars from him, and a price at which you would sell 20 cars to him.

The key additional questions that need to be answered before an offer can be made are: Where will you go if you get taken (if John buys cars from you)? How would you cover your short? (proceed to buy them back if you did not own any).

Convention in the bond markets is for a ¼ to a ½ per cent spread between bid and offer, depending on the liquidity of the issue. Using book price as your bid, a ¼, i.e. 0.25 per cent, spread between bid and offer would translate into a two-way price of $1,000,000 to $1,002,500. A spread of $2500 is very common in the bond markets, sometimes it is a lot less; a highly liquid bond may trade on a bid/offer spread of 0.03 per cent. $300 between the bid and offer on a face amount of one million bonds leaves little cushion for error. This is why traders have to be very thorough when doing their homework.

A trader must go through the car dealing type of thought process for every security he trades, constantly. In the same way as a car dealer may make two-way prices in BMWs, Jaguars, Mercedes, Rolls Royce, Granadas, Cavaliers, Ferraris, Nissans, Ladas, Trabants, etc., a bond trader who specializes in trading US Corporates for example, could be making markets in bonds issued by Exxon, Ford, GMAC, General Electric, Kelloggs, Pepsi, McDonalds, Procter and Gamble, i.e. corporations operating in many different industries. A trader who specializes in bank names may make markets in bonds issued by Barclays, BNP (Banque Nationale de Paris), Citicorp, Tokyo-Mitsubishi International plc, Deutsche Bank, Bank of Nova Scotia, etc.

Where trading takes place

The majority of trading in international securities takes place over the counter (OTC) which means via the telephone, or electronically. Securities can also be traded via an exchange, provided the security is listed on that particular exchange. Although the majority of eurobonds[1] are listed, usually either on the London or Luxembourg stock exchanges, some are not.

---

[1] *All further references to eurobonds in this chapter are to euro-currency bonds, i.e. eurobonds denominated in various currencies. The word 'currency' is dropped in general usage, as it is meaningless. In practice it is replaced with the specific currency of denomination, e.g. eurodollar, euro-Deutschemark, euroguilder, eurolira bonds, etc.*

A listing is supposed to ensure liquidity or at least provide an avenue via which one can obtain a fair idea of the price. In reality, very few bonds are traded on exchanges and thus the prices posted are rarely a good indication of the price at which business can actually be transacted. Nonetheless, some investor groups can only purchase listed securities. If a bond is unlisted it may not be as liquid.

Typical trading strategies

There are three main types of trading:

- outright directional trading
- spread trading
- arbitrage.

Directional trading involves buying or selling securities to reflect your view on the market, e.g. if a eurobond trader expected interest rates to go down, he may buy a big amount of liquid eurobonds, whereas if he expected rates to go up, he may sell short a big amount. In the same way, if he felt a particular security that he traded was undervalued, he may buy a lot of it, whereas if he felt it was overvalued, he may sell it short.

Spread trading involves betting on changes in the spread, i.e. the yield difference, between two securities or markets. This type of trading involves both a long and a short position. For example, a trader may go long of one security and short of another because he feels the spread relationship between the two is unusually wide or narrow. In the same way, a trader may go long of one market, German government bonds say, and short of another, Dutch government bonds perhaps, because he feels the difference in the spread between the two markets is out of line. Although there is risk, in that the spread could widen or narrow even further for reasons unknown to the trader at the time of trading, he does not need to have a definite view on where interest rates are heading to put on a spread trade, whereas he does if he is taking an outright long or short position.[1]

Arbitrage trading involves taking advantage of anomalies in price between the same or similar securities/markets. For instance, a trader may simultaneously buy and sell the same or equal securities in different markets, to take advantage of temporary aberrations in price. Arbitrage

---

[1] *See also 'Spread risk' and 'Yield curve risk' in Chapter 16*

trading is less risky than spread trading, but then so are the returns. The 'cash 'n carry' basis trade example in Chapter 17 is a typical arbitrage.

A trader usually operates on either a proprietary or market-making basis. As a market-maker, he must generate profit whilst providing liquidity to clients by supplying prices upon request. As a proprietary trader, he must generate profit, but is relieved of any obligation to deal with clients or competitors. Although a proprietary trader may, if he works for a firm that is a market-maker, show some of his trade ideas to certain clients, he is not obliged to do so.

When trading, a firm will usually act as principal which means it will use its own capital, and act as either the buyer or seller, i.e. the 'other side', of a trade. This tends to be the case even when a firm is acting as a broker and simultaneously buying from one client and selling to another.

Essential traits for successful trading

The key difference between a mediocre trader and a successful trader, is acceptance of responsibility combined with hard work. Traders often talk in terms of 'feel' or 'intuition' which, for some, can be wishful thinking, and for others, conviction based on effort. The latter is obviously preferred since it better ensures profit rather than loss. If you feel the market is going up, but it goes down, then you got it wrong and you must accept as much and make it your business to understand why. A mistake is not a sin, as long as you learn from it. In order to learn, however, you must first acknowledge that you erred. Some traders find this hard to do and may therefore blame other people or situations for their losses.

Any price a trader makes, must reflect his assessment of the collective psyche of all market operators involved. Accurately predicting thoughts, feelings, actions and reactions, and consciously seeking to influence them, is a critical part of a trader's job. To develop conviction with regard to the future price movement of a security or market, a trader must constantly ask questions of both himself and others, never forgetting that it is his personal responsibility to assess all of the answers and/or information extracted and to decide to what degree any of it should influence his price.

If you want to be a successful trader you must learn how to interpret information both swiftly and accurately. You must learn to identify risks and eliminate as many as possible, so you only take those that are necessary and which truly cannot be avoided. Good communication skills, a desire to win intelligently, and an awareness that the past need not be a precedent, are essential traits. The rest of this chapter examines your responsibilities as a trader, and introduces you to those questions that should be asked when trading.

How a trader determines the price of a security

As a trader it is important to have a view on where interest rates are heading, and the resulting effect this will have on the price of each security to be traded. Ideally, you should know the life history of every bond that you trade. In your efforts to make money there are numerous questions that must be asked, of both yourself and others. They are:

General market expectation questions

- What is the market consensus, and what are your own personal expectations for the currency and interest rates that directly impact your market?
- What is the general consensus, and what are your own personal expectations for all major currencies and interest rates that indirectly affect your market?

In addition to your own view, it is prudent to consult with other specialists such as foreign exchange traders, economists, and country analysts. Use all resources at your disposal. Where specialists exist, use them!

- What do your competitors think of the market?

Whether the Street is bullish or bearish is more easily assessed through direct conversation and price swapping. In the eurobond market, dealers can speak directly with each other, although much trading takes place via brokers. I personally favour direct contact. The tone of a person's voice can speak volumes. Nevertheless, brokers are useful when time and/or anonymity is of the essence. In any event, times are changing and the age of anonymous and instantaneous automated trading (see Chapter 7) is upon us. This will in some cases eliminate contact between competitors and consequently, traders will have to rely more on brokers prices and other prices displayed on screens, to gauge competitors' positions (see next question).

General supply/demand questions

- Overall, is the Street long or short?

Separating this question from the last one requires thought about whether competitors may be trying to talk the market up because they are long. If they sound bullish but you know they are long, maybe their bullish tone is more hope than conviction, which means they might just sell heavy into any rally. Traders judge Street positions from prices that other dealers make, the amount of—and reception to—recent new issues, as well as the level of enquiries and flow of business they are doing with genuine end investors.

• What do investors think, and do they have money to spend?

Notwithstanding the fact that investors are people who often change their minds, it is essential to obtain accurate information from sales colleagues about how clients regard the market. Are investors likely to buy, sell or hold, if the markets go up or down or do nothing? Since we often do not really know what we will do given a change until the change occurs, and since each client will look at life slightly differently, it is important to ask lots of questions so as to get as clear a picture as is possible about what could happen.

Specific supply/demand questions

The two critical supply/demand questions that must constantly be asked about each security you trade, are:

• Where will you go if you get hit (have to buy bonds)? What are your outlets?
• Where will you go if you get taken (have to sell bonds)? What are your sources of supply?

Should you be long or short in the bond? How does the bond compare to other comparable bonds and benchmarks? Is there an anomaly?

If a security is fundamentally attractive in terms of price and structure and therefore unswappable (e.g. there is no other security a client could sell against it and pick up yield in the process), it is unlikely that anyone will hit, even a high bid. In such cases your only source of supply might be the Street. Also, if the audience (investor base) for a particular structure or name is limited, it is not wise to go long (to buy) large amounts unless you can set a new price level through effective marketing. Setting a new price level on an historically-undervalued security requires a well-thought-out strategy, which usually involves a lot of time and effort on the part of many people. Such exercises can therefore prove a considerable drain on resources. There needs to be enough money in a trade to justify this sort of commitment.

Economic and political questions

• What is the economic situation like in the issuer's home country?
• Are there any wars or strikes or other impending disasters?
• What is happening politically?
• Is inflation under control?

Industry and company-specific questions

- Is the perception of the credit changing?
- Is anything going on in the issuer's industry that could affect their performance and profitability?

Perception is vitally important, irrespective of fundamentals. Inflation, strikes, political changes, wars, etc. affect fundamentals and sentiment, and in turn markets.

The last six questions are best answered by country and industry analysts and economists. If you do not have experts at your place of work, this sort of information is available from credit rating agencies. You should also read the newspapers and industry journals/magazines, and ask clients for their views and opinions.

New issue supply questions

- Is this borrower, or any comparable borrower, about to issue a new deal which could adversely affect the price of this security?

Check with your transaction desk and/or syndicate departments, as to their expectations in terms of upcoming supply. Even if your colleagues do not know, you will feel better having asked the question. Again, information on a country's or company's borrowing requirements can be found in newspapers, journals etc. Money for redemption of an existing security is also often raised by issuing a new deal. Information on upcoming redemptions is widely available from major wire services (e.g. Bloomberg, Telerate, Reuters).

Liquidity-specific questions

- What is liquidity like in the security?

Which other houses make a market in the bond? As a trader you are responsible for knowing Street and client liquidity levels for all issues that you trade. Liquidity levels change constantly (*see* 'Trading disciplines' later in this chapter).

- What prices are investors likely to be seeing away?

From speaking with competitors, brokers and clients, and from the prices available electronically on news screens, you should be able to get an idea of Street positions and therefore what other houses are likely to quote in a security.

Risk-management questions/considerations

- Could you hedge the security if necessary and if so, what other risks would you assume in the process?

If dealing in a US$ eurobond for example, you might use US Treasuries as a hedge although you would need to be very confident that the spread relationship will be maintained.[1]

- What are the financing costs?
- Is the bond available for borrowing and if so, what are the costs?

It is critical to know how much it costs to borrow money to buy securities. The finance desk will be able to supply this information and the repo traders or settlement staff will be able to tell you whether a bond is available for borrowing. You should know this information before, not after, being taken short.[2]

All of the above questions are intended as a checklist to be used as an alert to areas in which you should be well informed, and as a reminder of whom to consult.

Enthusiasm, energy, an inquisitive mind and belief in your own convictions are useful traits when trading. If you enjoy investigative work, and have a deep desire to win intelligently, then it is possible to become a very good trader.

You do not have to do it all or know it all. Just do and know more than the rest. In pursuit of becoming a successful trader, and to ensure that you achieve long-term success, read this book cover to cover. If you do not and a colleague or competitor does, you could find yourself at a disadvantage. The sales chapters in particular should be thoroughly read, as good trading requires a sound understanding of investors. Also, given that the majority of information you will require as a trader will come from other people, good communication skills are very important.

Facing up to losses

To succeed as a trader you must be able to cut your losses. To be prepared to get out whatever the cost, the moment things look bad. You must do this regardless of how it might affect the way in which you are perceived. Some

---

[1] *See 'Spread risk' and 'Yield curve risk' in Chapter 16.*
[2] *See 'Financing positions' in Chapter 13.*

traders find this hard to do, irrespective of social conditioning or academic background, because it involves a loss of face. If you find yourself hanging on, hoping, praying even, that the market will come your way, you could destroy your career.

If your image is more important to you than your obligations to your employer, trading is not the right career for you. The ability to cut a bad position at a loss is crucial if you want a successful career in trading. Doubling up never works. I know people who have done it and I know people who have been fired for doing it. The moment you find yourself even thinking about buying or selling significantly more of a security because your position is under water, recognize it as a symptom of your inability to take a loss. To hold on to a bad position is irresponsible, but to add to it in an attempt to push the price your way is reckless.

Even if you think you might lose your job if you liquidate at a loss, you must still do it. To hang on would be to put your personal interests above those of your firm. Any company that gives a trader the opportunity to carve a career for himself in trading, is risking their money and credibility on his behalf. For him to repay such an opportunity by trading irresponsibly with their money would be neither fair nor decent. The sooner you learn to deal with losses, the greater your chances of long term success.

Critical trading disciplines

When trading, it is vital to adhere to the following disciplines at all times.

General disciplines

- Create a master list with all relevant details on each bond that you trade, and add details of new deals as and when a new issue is launched. The information needed for this list is similar to that contained in our presentation sheets shown in Chapter 8 and is available from sources such as Bloomberg, Telerate and Reuters.

- Keep informed about liquidity levels and unborrowable securities. Stay abreast with which competitors trade which issues, especially those that you trade infrequently. It is essential to develop a sound procedure for deciding which issues to trade. It takes a lot of time and attention to keep track of just one bond, let alone an entire book, but nevertheless it is essential to be able to justify why you trade each of the securities that comprise your book. For example, your criteria should include all the information on the presentation sheet in chapter 8, as well as issue size, number of clients involved, and the number of market-makers. Since the last two points can change frequently, develop a procedure via which you can keep up to date.

- Monitor your P+L closely. Pay particular attention to financing, borrowing, fail and trade amendment costs, etc.

- Decide P+L targets ahead of time. Do not be too greedy. The Street is driven by greed and fear and, when things look bad, self-preservation. Understand the greed element and train yourself not to be too greedy. By holding out for the last cent, you could lose it all.

- Review your book constantly, but in any event at least once a day. Go over every position and ask yourself 'Why do I have this position?' Compare the value of each position with all other comparable securities in your market. If a better alternative exists, substitute. Always ask yourself the question 'If I was flat, would I choose to have this position?' If your answer is 'no', then cut the position immediately.

To reiterate:

- **Never hesitate to cut a bad position at a loss.**

Daily disciplines

- Know your positions at all times. Make absolutely certain of what your positions are before commencing the day's trading. Whilst it is the responsibility of clearance staff to help deal with settlement problems, it is not their job to know what you own or do not own. As a trader, always know exactly what your positions are.

- Decide early each day what needs to be bought and/or sold to reflect properly your current market view. Remember: the smaller your book is, the more objective you can be. What was cheap yesterday may not look cheap today. If a position is meaningless and can't be justified, then liquidate—and quickly.

- Look for what swaps/bids/offers make sense and distribute them on a standard form to salespeople. Check your notes and portfolios to see which customers might have an interest in buying what you want to sell or vice versa.

- Contact competitors to find out what is happening. Do not wait for other dealers to call first, especially if you sense activity taking place. Remember the bluff element. Regardless of whether you have a lot to buy and/or sell, by initiating calls you will be leading rather than following.

Last but not least:

- Always, always, always repeat every single detail of each trade back at time of execution. This includes whether you have bought or sold, and the full price. Write down each trade using an organized and simple format that suits you. Never operate on the assumption that your counterparty, be it a client or competitor, is talking about the same security.

In particular it is your responsibility as a trader to ask questions of salespeople, rather than to expect them to feed you every little bit of information about their clients' potential activities. Salespeople usually have a lot of clients to service.

Also remember, where appropriate, to split tickets when selling large amounts e.g. when selling one block of 20 million, split the trade into smaller pieces,[1] and do not forget that it is okay to ask for an order, and adjust your price for odd or unusually large amounts.

Tips for 'Street' trading

When dealing with competitors:

- Always make prices that suit you, and ask questions;
- Avoid becoming too friendly with people with whom you trade frequently;
- Never operate in concert with other houses;
- Never discuss client business or speak about a client by name;
- Never boast about your good trades.

When dealing with competitors it is sensible to keep your ears and eyes open and your mouth closed.

---

[1] *See Chapter 13.*

Chapter 7

GLOSSARY FOR CHAPTER 7

cap
The maximum payable in interest on a security. Sometimes a cap may only be in force for a certain period during a bond's life rather than for the whole of it.

Cedel
Based in Luxembourg, Cedel is one of the two largest clearing agents for international securities. The other is Euroclear, which is based in Brussels.

dealing price
The price at which one can buy or sell.

Euroclear
See **Cedel** above.

floor
The minimum interest payable. Some securities are issued with both a cap and floor which means that interest payments will always be within a certain range regardless of where actual interest rates might be.

Chapter 7

Risk control and automated trading: Technology in today's markets

Risk management and control

During the course of just one day, a firm may engage in thousands of transactions involving currency, interest rate and equity instruments in both the cash and derivative markets. Simply to finance its trading activities a firm must borrow, sometimes many billions of dollars each day from numerous different entities. This could include borrowing in one currency and then swapping into another in order to achieve the lowest cost. Each individual loan and any currency switch represents a transaction.

Many houses operate globally. With operations in every time zone and round-the-clock trading in numerous products one firm could therefore have 100 traders around the world, each buying and selling financial instruments in various currencies and with different structures. It is not uncommon for a single trader to transact business with 50 different counterparties (competitors and clients) on the same day, or for the number of individual transactions to exceed one hundred. During busy and volatile periods, it could be a lot more—ten transactions in five minutes for example.

Ensuring that each transaction settles on the due date requires highly efficient systems and procedures, so that funds and securities are available in the right currency, in the right place, at the right time. What amounts need to be paid or received and for whose account, and which securities are to be received or delivered—and for whose account—must be accurate. The creditworthiness of each counterparty must also be monitored on an ongoing basis.

Centralized agents such as Euroclear and Cedel, the two largest clearing organizations for international securities, make the settlement process relatively simple, and ISMA's transaction reporting and matching (TRAX) system has improved efficiency. However, for each individual transaction, the proceeds and delivery instructions must still be checked and agreed between all parties involved (*see also* Chapter 13). Any trade that is not entered into the system accurately, or on a timely basis, will therefore cause settlements staff both time and hassle. It will also distort the trader's positions and the firm's overall risk exposure.

If a few traders working for the same firm, for example, forget to enter trades involving large amounts of money and/or securities, their employers' risk exposure reports would be wrong by a substantial amount.

Few systems exist from which a single report, detailing the various risks resulting from all activities, can be created. This is not an ideal situation, but one which has emerged as a result of firms discovering, once involved in a product, that their existing system cannot handle the analysis of structure and/or the yield, interest or settlement calculations.

Whilst a single system could be designed and built internally, or purchased, it would be extremely costly, and the re-education of staff would involve a tremendous amount of time. Bespoke system(s) that are home-made, familiar and with flaws known, are unlikely to interrupt business in the way transferring to a new system could. Moreover, few firms would relish dependency upon an external source, over which they had a little to no control in terms of cost and design, but upon which the smooth running of their entire organization depended.

Whilst every house on the Street would like a system that could identify and analyse the risks inherent in all their outstanding transactions globally, and combine them in a single exposure report, this has yet to become reality.

Monitoring and managing, therefore, the various risks that result from capital market activities is a mammoth and complex task, especially when considering the sheer volume of transactions that can occur on one day. That said, any firm which does not have a quick way of finding out its overall market risk at any given time, is in a vulnerable position. The losses that can mount up on a bad position and go unnoticed for just one day, can be considerable.

It is also impossible to envisage a system that will protect a firm against an unscrupulous or tardy trader. The best deterrent for dishonesty is strict procedures (including appropriate consequences for violations which are consistently and rigorously enforced) combined with hands-on day to day management by experienced staff, supported by good systems. Even an efficient voice-recognition system that can analyse conversations, identify transactions, and discern inflection, will not deter an individual intent on exploitation.

Automated trading

OTC trading of international bonds already takes place electronically between individual participants; quotations are advertised and interested parties contact the dealer via telephone or e-mail to consummate a trade.

Some prices are 'firm' which means that the dealer is obliged to deal at the price quoted on the screen at the time of execution. Some however, are no more than indicative quotes and therefore subject to change. As a dealing price can differ a lot from an indication, it is prudent to ask whether a price is firm before divulging whether you want to buy or sell.

Automated trading within a regulatory framework is the next step. Automated systems already exist for currencies and shares but, as yet, no widely-used system exists for bonds in Europe. Tradepoint Investment Exchange, which began trading the leading 400 UK equities in August 1995, may however provide an opportunity.

The Tradepoint Investment Exchange is an order-driven, screen-based electronic market for securities trading, which offers institutional fund managers and broker dealers the opportunity of trading with each other, with equal and anonymous access to the market. Tradepoint became a Recognized Investment Exchange (RIE) in June 1995, which places it on the same regulatory level and ongoing surveillance, as the London Stock Exchange and LIFFE.

Tradepoint's structure involves an approved body acting as principal, i.e. the counterparty for all sellers and buyers. For UK equities this is the London Clearing House. As a result, counterparty risk is eliminated and the need for administration and technological support is reduced. As trading is instantaneous and automatic, and each transaction reported electronically to the buyer and seller, no transaction can get lost either! Although, at present, the Tradepoint system only handles equities, it is expected to be extended, as soon as feasible, to provide a mechanism for trading bonds in Europe. This will come to be welcomed by many institutions, particularly for the trading of liquid sectors of the government and eurobond markets, where there is already a high degree of transparency, and profits are now minuscule. For instance, large-size eurobonds with similar maturities, issued by borrowers of equally-excellent credit standing, trade much like a commodity.

Participant firms, be they broker dealers or institutional investors, will of course use the Tradepoint market to achieve their own goals, as they do any other market. For bigger investors that are extremely price sensitive, Tradepoint could offer timely access to a greater number of professional dealers as well as other investors. The Street would enjoy the same, and would also be able to deploy their experienced sales and trading staff in other more profitable pursuits.

For example, an experienced salesperson may call a client and engage in a long conversation about the markets. If he is lucky, the client may then want to do a trade: let us assume the client wants to sell US$25 million eurobonds. The trader's 'turn' on such a trade may be no more than 0.02 per cent (US$200 per million bonds, or a total profit of US$5,000).

Sometimes, a trader may make no profit but will be encouraged by the salesperson, in the interests of good relations and the potential to do better business in the future, to trade *at a wash* (for nothing) or, worse still, at a loss!

Anonymous trading would ease pressure on traders to engage in unprofitable business. Since there will be no personal connection, they will be able to choose whether they want to trade. Speculation that a relationship could be jeopardized will disappear.

Automated trading would enable investors and traders greater leeway, and more time to reflect on their respective needs and objectives. For example, the days of clients providing the Street with information on their market dealings in exchange for the very best prices available and extensive market/product research, could soon be over. Product/market research, which the Street has traditionally provided free to clients, as part of the overall service in its efforts to capture business, could be sold separately. Automated trading of bonds in Europe would add a new dimension and allow/require all users to be more innovative in their quest to make a profit. The swapping of market opinions for mutual benefit would, almost certainly continue, but obligations on traders to provide prices in addition, will be removed.

People inherently do not like change. But many believe that automated trading is a natural development which will enable the UK to maintain its premier position in the world of finance. A bond trading mechanism such as Tradepoint would offer investors and traders a choice, another route via which they can play the markets. The smartest minds with the deepest pockets, and the most courage, will have the most fun. But by far and away the biggest spin-off for such a system, will be the opportunity for traders and salespeople to use their valuable skills and experience, in more profitable and intellectually challenging ways.

The trading of illiquid securities

As a result of automated trading, experienced trading and sales staff would likely have more time to generate greater profit for their employers by dealing in less-liquid securities. Illiquid bonds could be traded via an automated market, but experience shows that the majority of transactions are the result of extensive analysis of structure and creditworthiness, as well as considerable dialogue, and many trades are often contingent on others. A client may only sell a capped floating-rate note issued by Mexico, for example, if a certain price can be achieved, and only then if a pre-specified alternative security that better suits their investment objectives can be purchased in replacement. *Reverse engineering*, which involves undoing the original structure and rearranging it to suit a client, may also be necessary. This could include, for example, re-arrangement of interest payments via an interest rate swap, inclusion of a cap and/or a floor, or a guarantee of a portion or all of the interest flows and/or principal by an unrelated party.

An indicative price can be displayed on a screen to test the water, to find out what the market price should be, and/or to find an entity that has opposite and complementing interest. However, this can also stir the market up and lead to nothing. Unless turnover is brisk in a security, and prices move within a narrow margin, a lot of homework must be done by a potential buyer. Generally speaking, if too many people know there is a potential seller of an illiquid security, the price usually goes down. If too many people know there is a buyer, it goes up. As a potential seller could dilute the chance of achieving their objective by advertising their intentions publicly, screens are rarely used for the purpose of transacting business in illiquid securities. Clients usually work discreetly with one house that has the necessary analytical, trading and distribution resources to accommodate their needs.

Experienced sales staff could also use their new-found freedom to service second tier (in terms of size) investors. Smaller institutional investors can benefit from, and are more likely therefore to value and reward, the expert advice and execution capability provided by a big house, particularly if they are not participants in an automated trading system. Whatever the reasons, any institution that is not receiving the optimum service available, but which is nonetheless of good credit standing, represents a potentially valuable client with whom mutually beneficial business can be done.[1]

---

[1] *See also Chapter 9.*

Chapter 8

GLOSSARY FOR CHAPTER 8

cover
The next best price.

'deal on the wire'
If a client is ready to 'deal on the wire' it means they are in a position to make a decision to buy or sell at that particular moment, and without the need to put down the telephone.

GTR
An abbreviation for guarantor. Some bond issues are explicitly guaranteed by, for example, a parent company or government. In some cases a guarantor may be a seemingly unrelated party. Bonds that are not specifically guaranteed are general unsecured obligations of the issuer.

outright or on swap
Refers to whether a client is buying or selling securities outright with new cash or because they need cash, or whether another transaction is involved. It is important to know where money is coming from, and where it is going, as it may represent another trading opportunity.

puts/calls
Many bonds contain a clause which give the issuer the right to call (buy back) some or all of the bonds prior to maturity, usually at certain times which are detailed in the prospectus at the time the issue is launched. A put gives the holder of the security the right to put (sell back) securities to the issuer. Some bonds have both puts and calls, usually exercisable at different times during a bond's life.

rating
A measurement of the perceived financial health and creditworthiness of a company, or country, as supplied by a rating agency. *See* **rating agency** in the Glossary for Chapter 6.

'...more behind'
Refers to whether a client or competitor has more business to do in a security beyond what they have divulged.

YTC
An abbreviation for *yield-to-call*. If a bond is callable by the issuer prior to the official maturity date its yield-to-call may be different from its yield-to-maturity, especially if the call price is different from the redemption price.

Chapter 8

Sales-trading relationships

Fights break out every day between traders and salespeople. The commonly-held view is that arguments cannot be avoided since often both clients and traders will be trying to do the same things in the market-place.

Some traders, when proposing ideas to their salesforce, provide only minimal information on the securities they are looking to buy, sell or swap, leaving the salesperson to collect all other details before calling clients.

Some salespeople, when asking for a market for a client, will often request a price without volunteering any more information about what their client might be looking to do, leaving the trader to ask a series of questions in his efforts to try and establish whether the client is looking to buy, sell or swap.

Both these situations waste time, cause arguments, and reduce the chances of doing good quality business with investors.

Traders often hesitate and then quote a wide price because of lack of information about the client. They may not know why they feel uncomfortable, but they do know that they are not entirely happy making a tight price.

Investors often hesitate and then lose interest in bids, offers or switch ideas because of a lack of information on the securities in question. They may not know what details are missing, but they do know that they do not feel convinced.

The interaction checklists at the end of this chapter, detail the information requirements of traders and salespeople. Whether trading or selling, if you endeavour to provide the information on these lists, it can help save time, reduce arguments, and make a positive contribution to increasing the flow and quality of business with investors. These lists include suggestions from other traders and salespeople who have attended workshops run by Euromarket Trading Consultants over the last eight years.

It is relevant to mention that salespeople can be very territorial, fearful that, if they divulge too much information, they will be more easily replaceable and less valuable to their employer. This is not necessarily so, although it is obviously a matter for individual judgement. If there are no firm-wide ground rules or a standardized approach in place at your firm, you need to be confident that your superior(s) will reward openness. My experience does not support the so-called wisdom of secrecy, though each case needs to be assessed separately.

In addition to using the interaction checklists, if you want to build good relations with trading or sales colleagues, there are a few things that must be avoided.

Responsibilities of a trader

Traders can damage relationships with sales colleagues and clients in many different ways, albeit inadvertently and unintentionally. The following are some basic ground rules for traders, borne out of experience.

- Never give an indicative price that is pure guesswork and which could be way off the market. To do so will embarrass sales colleagues and could damage the relationship with the client. It is better to explain that you have no idea.
- Never execute part of a client order with a competitor unless intending to confirm a full execution to the client. To do so can jeopardize the client's chances of completing what they have to do, and dilute your firm's credibility.
- Never sell bonds into the Street at a lower price than that at which you ask sales colleagues to sell them. If you sell bonds to a client, there is the potential to buy them back in the future.
- Accompany sales colleagues on client visits when possible. This will give an opportunity to learn more about the needs and concerns of customers, and strengthen your relationship with both sales colleagues and clients.

Responsibilities of a salesperson

Salespeople, too, can damage relationships with trading colleagues and put their employers capital at risk unnecessarily, without intention. The following are some basic ground rules for salespeople.

- Always tell your trader the name of your client.
- Always give feedback when your trader gives you a price. Do not treat, or allow clients to treat, your trader as a passive pricing service. If a client is reluctant to open up to you, ask some open questions. If it is a new client and you are treading gently, then tell your trader as much. To ask continually for prices without offering anything in return is exasperating for traders.

- Always find out by how much your trader won or lost when involving him in any competitive bid/offer situation. Even if your trader does the business, it is of great value to him to know the next best price (*the cover*) that your client obtained.
- Help traders to move difficult positions. There is always a price that works. Obtain counter bids and offers from your clients as to where they are willing to buy, sell or switch. Although your trader may not like the prices at which you can do business, at least he will know his downside if he needs, or wants, to liquidate.
- Invite traders on client visits when possible.
- Do not shy away from asking your traders simple questions for fear of looking stupid or being intimidated. If not clear on something, it is in your own interests to ask. If money or time is lost as a result of your having made assumptions, the '****' will really hit the fan, and you will get the blame. Some traders can be abrasive and arrogant, but this is why it is essential to ask all necessary questions. If you make a mistake that could have been avoided, the humiliation will be greater and there is no recourse.

Whether trading or selling, by making a conscious effort to work with sales/trading colleagues, you will learn a lot more about another aspect of your industry. This will make you more valuable as an employee, and more confident. You will also have someone to turn to for help.

Presentation of ideas

Whether a trader presenting market ideas to the salesforce, or a salesperson compiling information for clients on a bid, offer or swap, the use of pre-formatted sheets will save a lot of time, and eliminate the risk of forgetting a crucial detail which could adversely affect the merits of a trade. It also ensures consistency in your approach.

Figure 8.1 shows a miniature version of the format that I used when presenting bids, offers and swaps to sales colleagues. As well as the details shown, any useful selling points should be mentioned, plus any other information that may enhance your credibility.

Interaction checklist for traders

When proposing transactions to sales colleagues, a trader should provide the following information on each security to be bought or sold:

- Amount, name of issuer + coupon + full maturity;
- Price and yield;
- Spread relative to underlying government securities, if relevant;

- Details on puts/calls and any other wrinkles;
- Issue size and Street liquidity (i.e. number of dealers in the security);
- Rating, if any;
- What prices clients are likely to see away;
- Whether there is any flexibility in the proposed price;
- Whether a better execution could be achieved with an order;
- Whether a partial execution is possible.

Thereafter, the trader should provide:

- Immediate notification when a proposed transaction no longer works.

To both save time and increase the chances of getting a trade done, a trader could also provide information as to how a security was acquired, and its historical price performance relative to other comparable issues.

Interaction checklist for salespeople

When requesting a price, a salesperson should provide a trader with the following information:

- Name of client and whether the enquiry was unsolicited or initiated by him;
- Total amount in which the client is looking to trade;
- Full name of issuer and the coupon + maturity of the security;
- Whether the client is likely to deal there and then;
- Whether the client is dealing outright or on swap;
- Whether the client has already dealt or shown this business away;
- Whether it is a competitive bid/offer situation;
- Whether the client will leave an order or relax his price;
- Client's recent activity and general views on the market;
- Whether he has other clients involved/interested in the security and whether he could therefore help move a position should the client trade with him.

Thereafter, the salesperson should provide:

- Feedback on all prices given.

It is also helpful for a trader to know who his main competitors are in any given situation, as well as what a client is likely to do with the proceeds if it is an outright sale situation and, if an outright purchase, where the money came from.

	Amt	Issuer	Cpn	Maturity	Price	YTM	Call Date	Call Price	YTC	GTR	Issue Size	Rating
							Date	Price				
CS	5mm	XXX	9%	04/01/98	99 ⅛	9.14	1998	101	9.20	GG	100mm	AA+*
CB	5mm	ABC	9%	04/01/98	99%	9.16	N-C	N/A	N/A	GG	200mm	AAA

Date: Contact: US$ Desk

SUBJECT WE CAN BUY/SELL/DO THE FOLLOWING SWAP:

Selling Points

1) Pick-up yield/ Take-out $/ Upgrade credit

2) The non-call feature of ABC is a plus, given the quality of this borrower

3) Improve liquidity. There are seven market makers in ABC only three in XXX

We can do this trade in 1-5mm bonds, (partials okay). For additional we would like orders etc...

*XYZ has the option to convert to a floater at Libid minus 75bp, until next June.

Figure 8.1   Sample trade presentation sheet

Chapter 9

GLOSSARY FOR CHAPTER 9

debt
Debt obligation, the technical term for a bond.

illiquid
Refers to securities that are harder to buy or sell, i.e. bonds for which there are few or no registered market-makers. A bond can become illiquid for a variety of reasons, the most common being a deterioration in the creditworthiness of the issuer.

liquidity upside
A bond's potential to become more actively traded and therefore easier to buy and sell.

league-table
See subsection entitled 'League tables' in this chapter.

Triple-A rating
See **rating agency** in the Glossary for Chapter 6.

swaps market
Refers to the 'interest-rate' and 'currency' swaps markets.

well-rated
Refers to securities of good credit quality that are assigned a top rating by one of the big rating agencies. *See* **rating agency** in the Glossary for Chapter 6.

Chapter 9

Anomalies in the secondary markets: Determinants of price

Why anomalies arise

Since the eurobond markets are renowned for anomalies, it is important to know why they arise and why they will always exist.

Eurobond investors fall into one of three broad categories: risk-averse, risk-loving and somewhere in-between, as dictated by the nature of their business, their investment policy, and level of sophistication. In general, they do not take foreign-exchange risk, but stick to investment in securities denominated in currencies in which they have a natural flow of funds. Beyond this, however, which assets they will buy, and the amount of credit and liquidity risk they will take, varies within each investor group.

Whilst, in an ideal world, the preference is for bonds of the highest credit standing, such as sovereign debt or debt with a Triple-A rating, such investments are risk-averse and thus rarely provide adequate returns. Nor is there enough available in the right currencies and structures to satisfy overall demand. For this reason, there must be trade-offs between credit, structure and yield. While structure and currency can be altered via the swaps markets, straightforward natural assets are preferred because they are less cumbersome to purchase and more liquid thereafter.

Quite logically, investors prefer industries and names they understand most about, and structures that best complement their activities. Pension funds and insurance companies who, by their nature, have continuing cashflow liabilities, buy securities that provide them with known income streams over long periods, such as fixed-rate and zero-coupon bonds. Bank investors go for shorter-dated or floating-rate assets, where interest payments are pegged in some way to short-term interest rates, so as to complement the short-term nature of bank deposits. Certain floating-rate notes, for example, can therefore be attractive assets for banks because their coupons are pegged to Libor and adjusted periodically. Many banks simply participate to earn the 'spread' over Libor, by, say, borrowing money at Libor for six months and buying a floating-rate asset that provides a return of 6-month Libor plus something, although finding suitable assets for this purpose can be hard.

In terms of credit, and beyond the Triple-A rated sector, banks are more comfortable investing in the debt of other banks than corporations, since they understand the risks involved in banking and can more easily assess creditworthiness within that sector. Individuals, on the other hand, who collectively invest a lot of money in the eurobond markets, largely through Swiss banks, prefer household names, while central bank investors, usually only buy sovereign debt of the highest quality.

Like any market, the eurobond markets are very much driven by logical considerations. If we do not know a borrower, or its industry, or local economy very well, and there is no quick way to familiarize ourselves, then we are more likely to shy away from investing in its securities. Household names, therefore, tend to fair well, although name familiarity—through use of a manufacturer's product on a regular basis—can breed a false sense of security. Indeed, there have been cases where unrated 'household-name' borrowers manage to raise money on terms more fitting for a Triple-A rated issuer, while lesser known, but nonetheless highly credit-worthy, borrowers are unable to issue at economically-sensible terms because their name lacks familiarity among investors.

There are numerous other constraints which affect the price behaviour of eurobonds. Some investors for example, only invest a certain percentage of their portfolio in one particular name, and/or only buy a certain percentage of any one particular issue. They may also, due to liquidity concerns, only invest in issues of a certain size. However, small-sized issues of well-rated, known borrowers who do not come to the markets very often, are much sought after due to their scarcity value. Such issues bear up well in bad times and offer the potential for healthy capital gains in good times. Another consideration is the preference among investors for capital gain over a consistent income stream, or vice versa.

The above are just some of the reasons why the price behaviour of eurobonds can appear irrational. Given the diversity of the investor base, and the various criteria it uses to determine which investments are made, anomalies will always exist. That said, the dealing community also contributes to anomalies. While there are many thousands of issues that comprise the eurobond markets, only a fraction of these are actively traded.

This is due to lack of time and appropriate resources, as well as differing agendas. Whilst every house would, ideally, like to see the flows of business occurring in every market, many also want to maintain and/or enhance their league-table visibility, and devote a lot of money and resources to this end. This can lead to badly-priced new issues, as well as insufficient funds and staff for secondary market activities, both of which can erode liquidity and contribute to anomalies.

In the past, for example, there were numerous badly-priced new issues, some of which never recovered. A negative initial perception can deter both traders and investors from getting involved, and the issue can become known as a *dog*. Even today, if the market goes down following the launch of a tight deal, thereby making it unattractive at the *fixed price re-offer*,[1] the deal could remain in professional hands for a long time. If all the bonds end up back in the hands of the lead manager, the security could become tagged for life as a bad deal, and suffer a consequential lack of liquidity.

One concentrated, professional, 'forced' holder of a bond is no incentive to trade it, or invest in it. Although fixed price re-offer deals are designed to deter badly-priced issues, markets can and do change, and even correctly-priced issues can become dogs if, following launch, the market goes sharply lower.

As an aside, since the Street's objective is to actively trade securities rather than own a large amount of one deal until maturity, liquidation of dog deals usually takes place at some point. This can prove an excellent buying opportunity. It can be worthwhile, therefore, to keep track of new deals that do not meet with a warm reception. Providing the creditworthiness of the issuer is good—even if the bond is not liquid—if the price is low enough, the asset may be attractive as a core holding over the long term. I would also argue that too many investors concentrate on buying issues that are initially highly liquid, even though many often subsequently become illiquid. At least with initially-illiquid assets, there is the potential for the security to become more liquid, and go up in price.

Also, small-sized issues, and/or securities issued by unfamiliar entities, and/or issues with more complex structures, trade infrequently but require a lot of monitoring in the interim. Many houses lack the time and resources to trade these sectors, in terms of credit and product analysis, technological support and last, but not least, proven experienced trading and sales staff who can assess relative value.

The Street is no different from the investor community, except that its time horizon is much shorter. When determining which issues to trade, it favours larger, well-known and well-rated issues that enjoy broad investor appeal as it prefers a constant turnover, as well as—if it is engaged in mainstream primary markets—issues by borrowers who visit the markets on a regular basis. The net result is that there is considerable liquidity in a small number of eurobonds and virtually no liquidity in the rest.

---

[1] *See Chapter 10.*

Given the potential profit available from trading illiquid/less liquid securities, smaller firms that do not have major primary market ambitions can often be found to be niche players in a certain sector of a market. Bigger firms, however—especially those with major primary market activities and, in turn, extensive secondary market activities devoted to liquid securities—are faced with more of a dilemma and life for them can become a juggling act, as no individual firm has the resources to be involved in all sectors of all markets, all of the time.

Once you understand the psychology and constraints of both the investing community and the Street, the price behaviour of eurobonds can become quite predictable.

Chapter 10

GLOSSARY FOR CHAPTER 10

all-in cost
The cost, to an issuer, of raising money, usually expressed as an interest rate. For a syndicate manager 'all-in costs' usually mean interest payments and fees/commissions but not listing and other issuing expenses, such as legal fees, whereas an issuer may include all associated costs.

allotment
Allocation of new securities to syndicate members.

'in-syndicate'
When a new issue is in syndicate, it is in the process of being distributed to end-investors by those houses that comprise the syndicate group.

mandate
A binding instruction to proceed, as in a house receiving formal notification from a borrower that they have been awarded the mandate to lead manage their new issue.

market risk
Refers to the risk of a market going up or down as a result of movements in interest rates and/or changes in supply and demand.

Chapter 10

The primary market

<hr>

The primary market is the market where new issues are launched into the market-place. Up until the allotment date, a new issue is traded on a 'primary' basis. Once the lead manager has finalized allotments to each member of the syndicate, the issue goes 'secondary', and is then traded along with all other previously-issued securities in the secondary market.

Pricing new issues

Assessing and managing primary market risk is much the same as for the secondary market, but on a much larger scale. When pricing a new issue therefore, a syndicate manager must be very thorough when doing his homework. All the same questions as detailed in Chapter 6 apply, except that the risk is far greater. He could be buying 500 million or a billion dollars' worth of bonds, rather than just five million!

A syndicate manager usually bears ultimate responsibility for the price at which a new issue is brought to the market. He must therefore know, on an ongoing basis, which currencies, structures and names are in demand at any given time, and have a clear strategy in terms of which types of deals his firm wants to win.

While every house will want the mandate on a deal that is sellable, the Street can get carried away. When of lot new deals with unusual structures are being launched by competitors, the general assumption within houses that are not bringing in such deals, is invariably that there is a 'market', i.e. there is demand for them. History however proves that this is not always the case.[1] While there are various ways a deal can be structured, and an innovative structure may well prove the optimum route, this is not always the case either. The prospect of acting as lead manager of a sizeable new issue for a prestigious borrower has, in the past, bred some crazy structures under the guise of innovation, which ultimately proved unsellable. People

<hr>

[1] *See 'Avoiding disasters' in Chapter 21.*

can, and do, make mistakes—and even sophisticated houses can get carried away!

Constant dialogue with trading and sales staff is a key part of a syndicate manager's job. With the former, as to where comparable issues are trading in the secondary market, and with the latter, to ascertain the genuine level of investor demand.

Unless investor demand is being seen directly, and in sufficient size, it may not exist, and the market may simply be temporarily caught up in its own hype and a little disconnected with reality. As it can take a while to ascertain both the breadth and depth of investor interest in a particular product, a syndicate manager must, in the interim, be able to handle the inevitable pressure that can be brought to bear by borrowers, via corporate finance colleagues, who want to do deals. The corporate finance department will naturally want to write a ticket if at all possible, and will not be happy with the syndicate manager's refusal to provide a bid. In the absence of sufficient demand, however, it may be the only course of action if the employer's capital is to be protected.

When a syndicate manager is asked to bid on a new deal, the choices are: bid to miss, bid to win, or refuse to bid. If it is believed that a structure is not sellable and/or the terms the borrower is seeking to achieve are way too ambitious, a manager may decline to bid. To bid to miss is a more subtle way of refusing to bid. The other alternative is to bid to win, by the narrowest margin possible, so as not to bid too tightly (too close to the curve, e.g. 30bp off US Treasuries, rather than 32bp) and leave money on the table.

The needs and wants of borrowers

All borrowers want their desired amount of money in the currency and maturity of their choice, at the cheapest possible cost (cost being relative to market levels and what peer borrowers have been achieving). That said, they also want their deals to be perceived well and received positively by the press, well-distributed geographically with end-investors, and liquid in the secondary market. In short, they want it all.

When deciding which house they would like to take overall responsibility, i.e. lead manage their deal, borrowers will consider and (depending on their objectives) attach varying degrees of importance to a house's capital and primary market experience, foreign exchange, swap, and research capabilities, and its commitment to secondary market trading and distribution.

Frequent borrowers, those with ongoing needs for money, naturally want to do deals that maintain or enhance their image and thus ensure continued investor acceptance of their name. A lead manager will want this as well, but in addition to not instead of, making money and/or gaining league table visibility.[1]

Borrowers of the highest credit standing usually demand very tight terms, especially if they are unlikely to come to the market often. They know only too well how attractive their securities will be. Equally, there have been times when some firms have tried too hard to please borrowers at the expense of investors. Given that a borrower provides an opportunity for a house to lead manage an entire issue and thus write a very big single ticket, borrowers tend to be more revered than investors, as no single investor is likely to buy an entire deal and thus be as singly crucial to a transaction.

It should, however, be noted that while some borrowers may be a little ambitious in the terms they try to achieve, others may not know which questions to ask to ensure that they make the right choice in terms of how their deal is structured and priced, and which house should act as lead manager. Although some are highly sophisticated, others only come to the market occasionally and may therefore find it difficult to work out which type of deal to do, and with whom. This is particularly the case if a borrower solicits bids from too many houses, which can lead to them being deluged with proposals denominated in various currencies and with numerous different structures, swapped and twisted and tucked, so that it can be impossible to compare like with like.

A syndicate manager's job is both to question the merits of a chosen market, and to exercise creativity, by suggesting alternatives. While a borrower may request a bid in a particular currency and/or structure, it may be that a more economical alternative exists via another currency and/or structure. The syndicate manager that identifies such an alternative will naturally increase his firm's chances of winning the deal. The ability to think laterally is a key part of a syndicate manager's job. Both borrowing entities and the Street, can get locked into thinking about one particular route, when it may in fact make more economical sense to do something quite unexpected. Going against the grain can sometimes make all the difference.

There is also the press to worry about. No borrower will want to risk doing a deal on terms that are subsequently recorded as having been too generous. They could end up with very public egg on their face. They would also have the wrath of superiors and/or shareholders to deal with. Borrowers are people, and the majority are usually anxious to do a good

---

[1] *League tables are discussed later in this chapter.*

deal on fair terms. Borrowers with an over-inflated opinion of their standing (as in all life, there are always a few) can however, be both difficult to deal with and very demanding. This can cause a house to shy away from telling them the facts of life about what the market can take, for fear of losing a mandate. While the truth is always the best safeguard, it is not always welcomed initially. Usually however, it yields a good response once emotions quieten down.

Servicing borrowers

If you want a career in investment banking, it is important to understand that integral to your success will be an ability to convince borrowers—your clients—of the merits of issuing fairly-priced deals with structures that genuinely appeal to investors. Since a good relationship is a prerequisite, as is a complete understanding of investors, do read the sales chapter thoroughly. Make every effort because, unlike sales colleagues, you may only get one or two chances a year to write a ticket.

The syndicate group

A conventional syndicate comprises, in order of importance, a lead manager (possibly some co-lead managers as well), co-managers and underwriters, and selling group members.

The lead manager bears overall responsibility for ensuring that a deal is syndicated with competitors and distributed among investors in an orderly way, that maintains and/or enhances the borrowers standing in the market place.

Co-managers help with the orderly distribution of bonds to end-investors as well as underwrite (agree to buy) bonds up to the level of their participation, regardless of investor demand.

The selling group traditionally comprised investors, though nowadays one sees more professional houses than investors as selling group members. In the past, a selling group invitation would be sent to as many as 150 institutions, inviting them to subscribe for a very small amount of bonds. This enabled companies who only wished to participate in a minor way, to display (via the *tombstone* – a standard advertisement that goes into all major financial newspapers, and which lists every company involved in a transaction) their presence and interest in a particular market. Thus a selling group was a route through which investors could enjoy a little PR with minimal risk. These days, particularly in fixed price re-offer deals (FPR – discussed later), many professional houses act as selling group members, with each subscribing for quite large amounts.

League tables

The most prestigious role for any house is that of lead manager (which is also potentially the most profitable or the least expensive, depending on the market climate) because it is recorded in the league tables. League tables rank Street firms based on the number of deals they are involved in, and the capacity in which they participate, lead manager being the ultimate role. League tables exist for all major markets, both primary and secondary, though I would caution against viewing primary market league tables as a testimony of a firm's ability to manage and distribute large amounts of bonds. The Street however, does attach enormous importance to league tables and, from time to time, can suffer from league-table frenzy, particularly at the end of a year when two or more firms may be vying for the top position in the rankings and/or to surpass their main rivals.

For this reason, it is not uncommon to see a lot of new issues launched during the last week of December. There have also been cases where a house will indulge in the controversial practice of bringing a deal that is technically bona fide—and thus qualifies for inclusion in the league tables—but which, on closer examination is not, thereby exploiting the criteria via which league tables are determined. While the integrity of the tables for a market will depend on the integrity of its participants, there are some that take advantage of loopholes. Those who compile league tables, such as the IFR (*International Financing Review*) and *EuroWeek*, are constantly seeking to refine their approach. Since such practices do not directly affect any group materially, there is little more to say on the subject.

Where a deal has co-lead managers, the house on the 'top left' is the lead manager who 'runs the books', i.e. handles the accounts, and thus receives lead management credit in the league tables. The others receive co-lead credit which is not as prestigious. On very big issues the syndicate may include two categories of co-manager 'senior' and 'junior' determined by the size of their commitment.

Commission split among syndicate members

Commissions for new issues are based on maturity and credit standing. With the fixed price re-offer (FPR) approach, total commissions for AAA-rated borrowers or their equivalent, are generally ⅛ per cent for a 2-year deal, 3⁄16 per cent for a 3-year, a ¼ per cent for a 5-year deal, 0.30 per cent for a 7-year and 0.325 per cent for a 10-year deal.

In the 1980s, commission convention was 1⅜ per cent for a 3-year, 1⅝ per cent for a 5-year, 1⅞ per cent for a 7-year, and 2 per cent for a 10-year, although the term 'commission' became a real misnomer as mandates were awarded based on 'all-in cost', which included commissions.

For floating-rate note issues, however, commissions were changed to reflect reality a little better. There were numerous FRNs issued in 1985 and 1986 with tiny total commissions, in some cases 0.10 per cent (US$1,000 per one million face amount of US$ bonds), although many were still unsellable at, or within, total fees. As a result, the term 'profit' ceased to exist for a while as many deals were only sellable at, or in some cases in excess of total commissions. For instance, although total commissions on a 10-year deal might be two per cent, the bond might only be sellable (of value to investors) at less three per cent when compared to alternative securities available in the secondary market. A one per cent loss on just one million US dollar bonds is $10,000.

Foul play: a little history

To understand the logic behind the way new issues are brought to the market today, it is important to know something about the way things were.

The primary market is *the* market, i.e. the place where huge transactions that attract a lot of publicity and league table credit, take place. Because of this, during the 1980s, many houses which were relatively new to the markets, and which wanted to build a credible presence quickly, used it as their platform. Some spent vast sums of money bringing new issues to the market so as to establish themselves as a 'big player'. The logic was that if a house could attract business from one prestigious borrower they could lure others, as well as gain league table visibility, and in turn attract investors. However, many deals were loss-leaders. In these situations, a lead manager would take very few bonds itself, and distribute the bulk of the deal among the rest of the syndicate and therefore burden them with most of the losses. In many cases, the lead manager would not provide a supporting bid to the broker or, if they did, it would be at a price that represented a loss for syndicate members who wanted to liquidate.

On sellable deals, a lead manager usually provided a bid at, or just inside, total fees, so as to support the issue during its distribution to end investors. Although implicit in accepting an invitation to participate in a new issue, is an agreement to the proposed terms and a commitment to aid its orderly distribution to end-investors, many houses would accept invitations into deals which were unsellable at a profit. They would do this because they did not want to risk upsetting the borrower by declining and, in turn, being excluded from participating in future transactions.

It is also relevant to mention that some syndicate members, especially those new to the markets, would often sell their new issue allotment at any price, regardless of value. In the absence of a developed distribution network and, in their quest to develop a client base, this was a way to court favour with investors. For their part, investors would shop around for a weak syndicate member from whom they could buy bonds at the cheapest price. It was also common for firms with little or no access to investors, to accept an invitation and immediately liquidate their holding by hitting the first bid that appeared in the brokers market.

A select number of borrowers and investors did quite well during this period and took advantage of those houses willing to buy and sell at virtually any price. The rest of the investing and borrowing community, however, did not know what to make of the resulting erratic price movements. The combination of ill-priced deals, 'cut and run' games among syndicate members, and tactical investor restraint, led to a near total erosion of profitability and seriously diluted the credibility of the primary markets. All these shenanigans did little to inspire the confidence of either borrowers or investors, many of whom were either too confused or scared to participate. Something therefore had to be done about it, hence the introduction of the *fixed price re-offer*.

Fixed price re-offer (FPR) deals

The FPR is a relatively new approach via which new issues are launched into the marketplace. It is modelled on US primary market practice, and is now widely used for eurobond issues for well-respected borrowers. It was introduced to encourage better priced deals and in turn price stability, as well as to restore some level of profitability to primary market activities. So far the FPR is working, but its long term success will depend heavily on the extent to which market participants are prepared to stick together.

The characteristics of FPR

The characteristics of FPR are:

- Smaller total fees;
- Fewer houses in the syndicate who each take larger blocks of bonds and who commit to trade the securities in the secondary market;
- The period during which a deal is in syndication (launched and fully-syndicated) is very short; some deals are only 'in syndicate' for one hour;
- Pricing is in relation to underlying government bonds, or as an agreed yield with a specified coupon and set fees. This better ensures correct pricing;
- Where a selling group exists, it is likely to comprise Street firms who each take quite large amounts;
- When bonds are 'in syndicate', they can only be offered at the re-offered price which is set by the lead manager. This directive

prevents any syndicate participant from selling their allotment at a lower price than the rest of the syndicate group;

- IPMA do not recommend charging the syndicate group for stabilization costs and discourage charging a *praecipium*. A praecipium is a claw-back the lead manager can take from co-management fees, to reflect their extra effort.

Once the syndicate breaks, bonds are free to trade at prices that reflect genuine supply and demand.

Cost of bonds to members of the syndicate

A *lead manager* allots bonds to itself which they own at issue price, less the full fees, since they are acting in all capacities.

A *co-manager* owns bonds at issue price, less the co-management fee, the underwriting fee and the selling concession, plus any praecipium.

An *underwriter* owns bonds at issue price, less both the underwriting fee and the selling concession, although it is now rare to see a house acting purely as an underwriter as the risk is as great as that of a co-manager, but status and commission are both reduced. In days gone by, when the markets were developing and most deals were profitable, houses were far more anxious to be involved and would accept invitations to participate in whatever capacity was offered. Nowadays, however, a profit is far from guaranteed and houses are much more experienced, as well as more sensitive about where they appear on the tombstone *vis-à-vis* their peers.

A *selling group member* owns bonds at issue price, less the selling concession.

Block trades

A block trade involves a lead manager buying a new issue in its entirety. One reason a firm might take this approach occasionally, is because they expect yield levels to decline, and view the chance to win a mandate as both a buying opportunity and a way to achieve league table visibility. If a firm is eager to buy a deal and the borrower concerned is happy to allow that firm to 'go it alone', so to speak, there is no reason to stop them getting together. The lead managing house however would be assuming a lot of risk, as it could end up owning all the bonds!

If the deal proves unsellable and is difficult to hedge and/or if the creditworthiness of the borrower deteriorates, they could lose a lot of money. Block trades can also be the result of a house, in its quest for league table credit, bidding for a deal way too expensively. In other words, buying it, and then trying—but failing—to form a syndicate. Where a new issue appears, either without a syndicate group or one that is very small, it could mean that the deal is extremely attractive and the lead managing house wants as many bonds as possible for itself, or alternatively, that the deal is extremely unattractive and no one wants to participate.

Seasoning

Although there are exceptions,[1] the SEC (Securities and Exchange Commission) does not allow US investors to buy non-SEC registered securities until the initial offering of securities are *seasoned*. This is usually after a prescribed period of 40 days following the payment date. However, any original unsold allotments must be sold to European investors before they can become seasoned. This encourages borrowers to use the US markets directly if they want to access funds held by US investors, and it also protects US investors from buying international securities that may not be sellable in Europe.

A new offering may also be subject to sales restrictions in the country of the issuer, the guarantor, or the currency. Check for sales restrictions before buying a new issue.

Global bonds

The first global bond[2] was launched by the World Bank in September 1989: US$1.5 billion of 10-year notes. The World Bank, a supranational entity with on-going financing needs, pioneered the concept to access investor funds, both in the US domestic—as well as international—markets, in a timely and cost-efficient way. Pricing is based on US domestic market yield levels but, because distribution is broader, the issue size can generally be much larger than for a conventional US domestic or traditional eurobond offering. Global offerings are not subject to seasoning requirements. Given their larger issue size, they are usually very liquid. Prices tend to move within a relatively narrow range and follow movements in the US government markets. Global bonds can therefore be used for short-term

---

[1] *US investors may be able to buy a new international offering, subject to criteria prescribed by the SEC. The securities however, would have to be registered and would remain registered for life and not fungible, therefore, with any remaining bearer securities. The lack of fungibility would be reflected in the secondary market price. Consult a legal expert on US sales restrictions before selling unseasoned securities to US investors.*

[2] *Although there have been simultaneous offerings of securities in both the US and internationally, this does not constitute a global bond, because issuing and settlement procedures are different for each tranche.*

interest rate speculation, as well as long term investment purposes and repo market activities, in much the same way as liquid government securities.

Common terms used in new issuance

The following are common terms to be found in relation to new issues. A brief description of each is provided though refinements will exist. Consult legal staff for an expert opinion.

■ Negative pledge
This clause ensures that the claims of bond holders are not inferior to the claims of other creditors upon liquidation.

■ Cross default
An event of default is deemed to have occurred when other bonds or loans are in default, i.e. where one bond is declared in default all other similar bonds are also in default. Default can be triggered by non-payment of interest or principal by a borrower, or some other event which enables lenders to take action before non-payment occurs.

■ *Pari passu*
This ensures that any other unsecured bonds (of the same type) will rank equally in the event of a default and subsequent liquidation.

■ *Force majeure*
This protects against any significant event that might occur between the launch of a new issue and the payment date. For example, if war broke out in the country of the issuer, participation could be withdrawn.

Chapter 11

GLOSSARY FOR CHAPTER 11

fixed currency
Where the exchange rate between two or more currencies is not allowed to move up and down freely, but is controlled by a central bank or a group of central banks via a prescribed formula, usually for the purposes of providing economic stability.

free-floating currency
The opposite of the above, where exchange rates move freely based on supply and demand, i.e. the amounts bought and sold relative to other currencies.

Chapter 11

Waiting for the figure

Economic and financial statistics (the *figures*) are important because they provide an idea about future changes in interest rates and exchange rates. There are hundreds of statistics published constantly. Those included in this chapter are the most closely-watched by the market and, while some of those mentioned are always important, others are only important from time to time, depending on the state of the economy.

Publication times vary from country to country, but the same statistic is usually released with the same frequency—usually weekly, monthly or quarterly. The same statistic can also have a different name in different countries (for example, American *consumer price inflation,* or CPI, is British *retail price inflation,* or RPI).

Because of the time it takes to compile statistics, when new, they usually relate to an earlier period rather than to the immediately preceding week, month or quarter. Also, once a number is released, it is often revised and modified.

There is much debate and discussion among economists about what a number means and how good a measure it is of the item in question. However, at any time, we have to trust that, whatever the figure, it is the best possible measure available of what it is supposed to represent.

The key question when a figure is released is: 'is it good for the market, or bad for the market?'. If inflation is rising, then interest rates will rise to keep real returns the same, in which case bond prices will go down. If the yield on bonds (i.e. government bonds, which reflect the state of the economy) is seven per cent, but the inflation rate is running at three per cent, then the *real return* is (seven minus three) per cent, i.e. four per cent. Conversely, if inflation is falling, bond prices will go up.

What is most critical is not the actual number, but the difference between the number and market expectations. If a figure released is not as bad as expected, then even if overall it is an indication of rising inflation, the market may still go up if in the run-up to release of the figure, prices were adjusted downward to reflect a worse number. Whether a figure will push prices up or down will depend on the extent to which the market may have already factored in a particular number. The relevance of figures published at any time is related to how worried the markets are about inflation and the extent to which the figures clarify or pinpoint a particular trend. Figures most affect the market when they suggest some sort of change from the present trend.

There are no hard and fast rules as to what is important at any time as the whole market is in a constant state of change, but a stream of reasonably consistent numbers provide security in that they become predictable. It is when a number that surprises the markets comes out, that the most buying or selling occurs.

To get a clear idea of what numbers are important, it is necessary to remember why inflation occurs and when it may rise. Inflation occurs when demand for goods exceeds supply—when people (governments, corporations and individual consumers) want to spend on goods at a faster rate than goods can be produced. The result is either that prices start rising faster leading to inflation, or that there is a 'sucking-in' of imports from abroad, leading to a worsening balance of payments (also known as *current account*, or *trade deficit*).

Whilst a balance of payments deficit may exist, it is not a desirable state for a country to be in over a long period. It will have to borrow money or use its foreign currency reserves in order to meet the shortfall. This leads in the end to a decline in the currency.

On an individual level, you know it is not sensible to live above your means—to spend more than you earn. To do so continually, would mean ending up heavily in debt and dependent on loans from others. Interest charges would require you to earn more just to stand still, your credibility to manage your financial affairs would diminish, and you would eventually be bankrupt. If, for example, you had your own personal currency that was used to settle debts, how many others do you think, would want a surplus supply of it as part of their foreign reserves, or want to own securities denominated in it? To remain debt-free, the sum total of all your purchases of goods and services must always equal what you are able to produce, i.e. what you are capable of generating in income.

As a currency gets weaker, the cost of purchasing abroad goes up. Whether one is purchasing raw materials or final products, any increase in cost is ultimately passed to consumers, which can lead to inflation.

All countries are therefore constantly striving to achieve the ideal situation—where demand equals supply perfectly, or where the value of exports matches or surpasses the cost of imports.

Incidentally, the manifestation of a currency decline will depend on whether the currency is *fixed* or *free-floating*. The collapse of sterling in September 1992 was preceded by massive intervention from the Bank of England, and when it came was quite dramatic because sterling was a member of the European exchange rate mechanism (ERM). By contrast, the fall of over 20 per cent in the value of the US dollar against the Japanese yen in the first three months of 1995, was steadier because both currencies were in a free-floating relationship. Which is better depends on who you ask!

As well as banks, corporations and consumers, the main borrower in any domestic market will be the government—hence the importance of a country's deficit or borrowing requirements. While a government could fund itself in the short term by simply printing money, as with the balance of payments, this couldn't go on forever because of the inflationary implications. The money would become worthless.

The figures to watch

The figures to watch, and what they measure, are as follows:

OUTPUT AND PRODUCTION

These statistics...	*measure changes in...*
Gross domestic (or national) product:	The total value of goods and services produced in the economy
Manufacturing/industrial production:	Output from factories and utilities
Capacity utilization:	Utilization of equipment/machinery
Unit labour costs:	The labour costs of producing an item

DEMAND

These statistics...	*measure changes in...*
Retail sales	Sales of goods and services by product
Consumer spending	Total amount spent on the above
Consumer credit	The number of applications for credit
Balance of payments	Import costs vs. income from exports
Money supply (demand for credit)	Amount of money in circulation

There are various measures of money supply. The narrowest is M0 which measures notes and coins in circulation. M1 (also M1 in the US) measures cash and money held in cheque (current accounts), while M2 measures the amount of money held in interest-bearing accounts, as well as other short-term cash substitutes, such as money market funds.

Central banks can temporarily control the amount of money in circulation by engaging in repo and reverse repo transactions. A repo injects money into the banking system, and involves the government buying Treasury bills. A reverse repo involves the government selling bills, thereby draining money out of the system. If you hear *system repos* announced over the 'squawk box', it is usually good for the market, since it indicates that the central bank does not want interest rates to go up, which would occur if the demand for money exceeded its supply. Conversely, if you hear *reverses* announced, it is a sign that short-term interest rates could be on the way up.

PRICE RISES

These statistics...	*measure changes in...*
Consumer (retail) price inflation	Living costs. e.g. food, clothing, accommodation (mortgage payments) petrol, heat, light etc.
Producer (wholesale) prices	The cost of goods and services before mark-up for retail distribution.
Commodity prices	The cost of raw materials and produce i.e. coffee, tea, sugar, wheat, corn, pork bellies, oil, copper, aluminium etc.
Wage rises	This one is self-explanatory. The theory is that if wages rise too quickly, and too much money is the system chasing too few goods, then inflation will occur.

UNEMPLOYMENT

These statistics...	*measure changes in...*
Unemployment rate	Unemployment levels.
Jobless claims	The number of people claiming benefit due to falling out of work.
Employment levels	The number of people employed in the economy.
Leading Economic Indicators (LEI)	This is a closely-watched statistic. It is a composite index designed by governments to anticipate changes in economic cycles, and thus it comprises those statistics that serve as the earliest warnings of change.

The LEI index comprises statistics which have proven to be the most reliable barometers of economic changes in the future. These include orders for plant and machinery, housing development applications, new business start-ups, purchasing managers surveys (where buyers across the spectrum are asked about their spending plans), overtime hours, inventory levels, delivery times, money supply etc.

The markets engage in a ritual building up to release of figures. Many economists publish their forecasts, which can vary dramatically. The consensus view is then published, and this can either be the average of all forecasts, or the median (the one right in the middle of them all). This can usually be found in such publications as *Money Market Services*. You can compare your economist's view with market estimates, all of which can change, particularly as other figures are published. For example, capacity utilization can help in gauging industrial output. If the economy is emerging from recession, and capacity utilization is higher than expected, manufacturing/industrial output is likely to increase, which could lead to an increase in the number of jobs which, in turn, could mean a downward revision of the unemployment rate.

There are more to the figures published than the 'headline' figure which first appears on news screens. The key is to know when a number is reaching the point when it signals inflation or recession.

As soon as a figure is released, economists will look behind it at the details. This is particularly important, as there can frequently be special factors which distort a figure. For example, trade figures can be especially affected by one-off imports or exports of single large items, such as aircraft, or by goods which are just 'passing through', such as precious stones. Or else, there can be revisions to the previous months' figure, or a series of previous figures if a much earlier one is found to have been inaccurate. Seasonal swings are usually taken into account, so that a number is announced as 'seasonally adjusted'. For instance, unemployment usually falls during holiday periods when temporary staff are employed to enable permanent staff to go on vacation. The point to remember is that a seemingly innocuous figure can, in fact, have a long-term degree of relevance, whilst the opposite can also be true.

Economic figures exist to help us assess long-term trends. While some figures are always important, others, such as capacity utilization, are only relevant when the economy is verging on overheating or falling into recession. Your economist, and economic forecasts published in the press, will highlight what is of relevance at any particular time, so that you are not caught by surprise.

Whether a figure was, in fact, heralding a change in long-term perceptions or was an exceptional 'blip' can take several months to confirm. Surprise numbers in particular, need to be analysed and understood.

To summarize, waiting for the figure can be regarded as a process which has five stages:

1) Checking the timetable of figures to be published for the month;
2) Comparing market expectations with your own;
3) Monitoring the extent to which the market is adjusting up or down in price for a good or bad figure, ahead of its publication;
4) The actual publication of the figures and the initial reaction;
5) The reaction of the market after more careful economic assessment.

While a market may react significantly in the run-up to a figure it can then stop dead in its tracks or even reverse, once the figure is released and its implications understood. Panic-trading immediately after a figure is released can, in hindsight, turn out to be costly and unnecessary.

For a trader, it is crucial to stay in touch, via salespeople, with clients. Investors in a market are the biggest and best barometer of where that

112

market is heading. If a trader asks the right questions of the right type of investors, he will have the best idea of what will happen to his market after a figure is released. You should also watch out for central bank or Fed meetings, speeches by central bankers and politicians, and other political or economic events.[1]

If you would like to learn more about economic indicators I would recommend *The Investor's Guide to Economic Indicators* by Charles R. Nelson.[2]

[1] *See 'Trading' in Chapter 6.*
[2] *See Bibliography for full details.*

Chapter 12

GLOSSARY FOR CHAPTER 12

actual/360 or 365
Refers to interest payments that are calculated based on actual days lapsed divided by either 360 or 365 days.

counterparty
The person or entity with whom you deal and who therefore represents the opposite part of a transaction, i.e. the 'other side' of a trade.

settlement date
See **clearance** in the Glossary for Chapter 3.

Chapter 12

Interest calculations and conversions

Eurobonds

If you borrow one million dollars at 8 per cent for one year, you will pay $81,111.11 in interest (1mm x 0.08 / 360 x 365). If you then use this money to buy a eurobond with a 8 per cent coupon at a price of 100 (par), you will only receive $80,000.00 interest (1mm x 0.08). This is because interest on eurobonds is calculated 360/360. It is assumed that each year only has 360 days and each month 30 days. This represents a saving for borrowers of five or six days interest per year, which can be considerable on a big size issue, particularly in a high-interest rate environment. You may also find that the maturity date on some issues is designed to fall on a Saturday which, since repayment can only take place on a business day, can save a borrower another two days' interest.

On secondary market trades where the profit margin is small, day-count differences can wipe out any gain. This is best illustrated using the month of February.

Example ➤

Assume that, on 25 February, you sell 1mm of a eurobond with a 9 per cent coupon and a coupon payment date of 15 February, at a price of 100.* Regular settlement will be on 28 February and the proceeds of this transaction would be as follows:

Principal	$1,000,000
+ 13 days' A/I**	$3,250
Total proceeds	$1,003,250

* *The date upon which coupons fall due for payment throughout the life of a security is usually—in the case of eurobonds, which pay interest annually—the same month and day upon which repayment of principal is to be made when the bond matures, providing such day is a 'good business day'. Otherwise payment is usually made on the next good business day thereafter. For instance, a bond that matures on 15 December 2005, will usually pay interest on that same date.*

** *Accrued interest (interest which accrues between coupon payments) is calculated from the day following the last coupon payment date up to and including the settlement date.*

If, however, you were to sell these same bonds on 26 February, regular settlement will be on 1 March and, because the month of February is assumed to have 30 days, the proceeds would be:

Principal	$1,000,000
+ 16 days A/I	$ 4,000
Total proceeds:	$1,004,000

After deducting one day's accrued interest, to take into account that you dealt on 26 February rather than 25 February, would produce a gain of $500.00 if you were the seller. If, however, you were the buyer, you would lose $500.00. When buying bonds on 25 February, if a counterparty asks you to extend settlement by one day from 28 February to 1 March, you will know why—and also to say 'no'. This is not to suggest that you spend a lot of time focusing on the day count of bonds at the expense of trading—rather that there is a difference which, on marginal trades, could affect your decision.

Money market instruments

The day count convention in the money markets, which includes cash loans and deposits and short-term instruments, differs not only from country to country, but also from instrument to instrument. It is usually actual/360 or

Australia	actual/365	Japan	actual/360
Austria	actual/360	Netherlands	actual/360
Belgium	actual/365*	New Zealand	actual/365
Canada	actual/365	Norway	actual/360, under one month; 30/360 over one month;
Denmark	actual/360	Sweden	30/360
Ireland	actual/365	Switzerland	actual/360; Federal bills: 30/360
Italy	actual/360	United Kingdom	actual/365
France	actual/360	United States	actual/360
Germany	actual/360		

In Belgium, although domestic convention is actual/365, in the international markets actual/360 is sometimes used on Belgian franc instruments.

Figure 12.1   Country day count convention

actual/365. International money market securities often follow domestic convention. Figure 12.1 shows the conventions most frequently used in the major markets.

Where interest is calculated actual/360, a security will pay interest on the actual number of days elapsed: either 365 or 366 days. Unlike fixed-rate eurobonds, therefore, no interest is 'lost'. For example, if you invest US$1,000,000 in a CD for one year at a yield of 9 per cent and US$1,000,000 in a eurobond for one year at a yield of 9⅛ per cent, you will receive the same amount in interest on each security (unless it is a leap year).

On the CD, interest would be calculated actual/360 and you would receive $91,250 ($1,000,000 x 0.09 x 365 / 360), or $91,500 in a leap year. On the eurobond, interest would be calculated 30/360 and you would also receive $91,250 ($1,000,000 x 0.09125 x 360 / 360 = $91,250.00).

Floating-rate notes (FRNs)

Interest on euro-FRNs is calculated actual/360. FRNs are often pegged to Libor, the short-term cost of funds for banks, upon which interest is also calculated actual/360.[1]

Converting yields from one interest basis to another

To find the money market equivalent of a eurobond yield, multiply by 360 and divide by 365. To find the eurobond equivalent of a money market yield multiply by 365 and divide by 360; or use factors derived from 360/365 and 365/360.

Finding annual and semi-annual equivalent yields

US government securities pay interest semi-annually on an actual/actual basis. Eurobonds usually pay interest annually on a 30/360 basis. One way of assessing the value of a eurobond denominated in US dollars, is to compare its yield with that of a US government security with the same or a similar maturity. To enable comparison, however, the yield of each security needs to be expressed in the same way.

The formula for finding the equivalent annual yield of a semi-annual yield is:

---

[1] Except *eurosterling FRNs which pay interest actual/365. However, as interest for sterling borrowings is calculated actual/365, the convention is the same as that used for non-sterling FRNs.*

$$\text{annual yield} = [1 + (\frac{SA}{2})]^2 - 1$$

where,

SA   is the semi-annual yield expressed as a decimal.

Thus, the equivalent annual yield of an 8 ⅝ per cent semi-annual yield is 8.81 per cent:

$$AY = [(1.043125) \times (1.043125)] - 1 = 0.0881 \text{ or } 8.81\%$$

Cross check

Investing 1000 for one year at 8⅝ per cent semi-annually, produces interest of 43.125 (1,000 x 0.08625 x 180 / 360) after six months. The first semi-annual coupon payment of 43.125 is assumed to be reinvested at 8⅝ per cent for a further six months, resulting in additional interest or 'interest on interest' of 1.86. Thus, the first coupon payment of 43.125 grows to 44.98 which, added to final six months' coupon payment of 43.125, equals a total return for the year of 88.10.

The semi-annual equivalent of a 12 per cent annual yield is 11.66 per cent:

$$\text{semi–annual yield} = 2[(\sqrt{1 + A}) - 1]$$

$$\text{semi–annual yield} = 2[(\sqrt{1.12}) - 1] = 0.1166 \text{ or } 11.66\%$$

Find therefore, the square root ($\sqrt{\ }$) of 1 plus the annual yield, deduct 1, and then multiply by 2.

In case you are wondering, there is no formula for converting interest paid on an actual/actual basis to a 360/360 basis when dealing with a one-year period. While there will be a difference in accrued interest for periods of less than one year, for a whole year the amounts would be the same.

Discount securities - converting a discount rate to an equivalent yield

Discount securities, such as commercial paper, bankers acceptances and Treasury bills, are issued at a discount to their redemption price. They are similar to zero-coupon bonds, except that they have short maturities and interest is usually calculated actual/360, rather than 360/360 or actual/365. Since these instruments are quoted and traded at a discount to par, to be able to compare their value with a short-dated eurobond or coupon-bearing money market instrument such as a CD, the discount rate must be converted into an equivalent yield.

Equivalent money market yield

The formula for finding the equivalent money-market yield (*mmy*) of a discount security is:

$$mmy = \frac{360d}{360} - dt$$

where,

d   discount rate
t   days from settlement to maturity

Example ➤
The equivalent money market yield of a discount security trading at a 5 per cent discount with 182 days from settlement to maturity is 5.13 per cent.

$$mmy = \frac{(360 \times 0.05)}{(360 - (0.05 \times 182))} = \frac{18}{(360 - 9.1)}$$

Step One: 360 x 0.050 = 18
Step Two: 360 - (0.050 x 182) = 360 minus 9.1 = 350.9
Step Three: 18.0/350.9 = 0.0513 or **5.13%**

Equivalent eurobond yield

To calculate the equivalent eurobond yield, change the formula to reflect the day count difference between eurobonds and money market securities:

$$\text{eurobond equivalent yield} = \frac{365d}{360} - dt$$

If you know a discount rate's money market equivalent yield, you can also find its eurobond equivalent yield by multiplying by 365 and dividing by 360:

$$5.13\% \times \frac{365}{360} = 5.20\%$$

120

Annual to semi-annual			Semi-annual to annual		
Annual to	*Semi*	*Basis point difference*	*Semi to*	*Annual*	*Basis point difference*
%	%		%	%	
2	1.99	1	2	2.01	1
3	2.98	2	3	3.02	2
4	3.96	4	4	4.04	4
5	4.94	6	5	5.06	6
6	5.91	9	6	6.09	9
7	6.88	12	7	7.12	12
8	7.85	15	8	8.16	16
9	8.81	19	9	9.20	20
10	9.76	24	10	10.25	25
11	10.71	29	11	11.30	30
12	11.66	34	12	12.36	36
13	12.60	40	13	13.42	42
14	13.54	46	14	14.49	49
15	14.48	52	15	15.56	56
16	15.41	59	16	16.64	64
17	16.33	67	17	17.72	72
18	17.26	74	18	18.81	81
19	18.17	83	19	19.90	90
20	19.09	91	20	21.00	100

$$\text{Annual yield} = [1 + (\tfrac{i}{n})]^n - 1$$

Where i is the semi-annual yield expressed as a decimal and n is the compounding frequency

E.g. to find the annual equivalent of an 8 per cent semi-annual yield, input into your calculator 0.08 / 2 + 1, then multiply the result by itself and subtract 1 to arrive at the annual yield equivalent, which is 8.16 per cent. Alternatively, you could halve the semi-annual yield, square it and add the result to the semi-annual yield.

$$\text{Semi-annual yield} = 2\,[\,\sqrt{(1 + A)} - 1]$$

E.g. to find the equivalent semi-annual yield of a 10 per cent annual yield, input into your calculator 1.10 then press the $\sqrt{\ }$ sign, subtract 1 and multiply by 2 to arrive at the semi-annual yield, which is 9.76 per cent.

Figure 12.2   Conversion of semi-annual and annual yields.

Summary

- Interest calculations on cash borrowings in a currency are usually the ones used to calculate interest on money-market instruments in that currency. This is usually actual/360 or actual/365;
- Interest calculations on international money market products usually, but not always, follow domestic conventions;
- Interest calculations on discount securities are usually calculated actual/360;
- Interest on euro-FRNs is usually calculated actual/360, but interest on eurosterling FRNs is calculated actual/365;
- Interest on eurobonds is usually calculated 30/360;
- Interest on repos (*see* Chapter 13) is usually calculated actual/360.

It is important to check how interest is calculated when borrowing money to buy bonds, or comparing the value of two securities with different structures. When buying or selling a security part-way through an interest period, it is also important to understand how accrued interest (which is always payable to the seller) is calculated, as this will affect the proceeds of a transaction.

Note: US Treasury bills usually only pay 364 days interest per year.

Chapter 13

GLOSSARY FOR CHAPTER 13

full price
The net price plus accrued interest.

mm
An abbreviation for million

net price
The price of a bond net of accrued interest.

partial delivery
The delivery of a portion, but not all, of the securities contracted to be delivered. Note a partial delivery can be refused by the buyer unless partial delivery was agreed at the time of execution.

positive/negative carry
The cost of financing securities held in inventory after allowing for coupon income on long positions and loss of coupon income on short positions. Any gain derived from holding or carrying a security is known as *positive carry* while any loss is known as *negative carry*.

trade date
The date when a transaction is executed.

Chapter 13

Financing positions

The value of a firm's inventory changes daily, and is generally multiples of its capital. A house with US$3 billion in capital could have trading positions with a total value in excess of US$100 billion! Street firms therefore, need to borrow money every day—and in many different currencies. Finance departments are responsible for doing much of this, by raising money at the cheapest possible cost to support their employer's trading activities. They also takes care of borrowing securities to satisfy the short sales of trading colleagues. The borrowing and lending of securities is often done via the repo market (which is discussed later). This chapter looks at financing from a bond trader's perspective.

The normal settlement[1] of international securities is three business days following the trade date. When a trader buys a bond, he must borrow money to pay for it. Interest charges on money borrowed will be partially, or fully, offset by the coupon income of the security purchased.

When a trader sells a bond that he does not have in inventory, it will have to be borrowed, so as to be delivered on the settlement date. If a bond cannot be borrowed, the trader will incur the full coupon cost for each day it is not delivered.

For the following examples an overnight financing rate of eight per cent is used, which is equivalent to 8.11 per cent on a eurobond basis.[2] This is the rate at which the majority of traders can borrow money to finance their positions, i.e. pay for purchases of securities.

Financing long positions

On long eurobond positions the trader:

    GAINS coupon income x par amount
    LOSES financing rate x amount borrowed (principal + A/I)

---

[1] *Settlement is discussed in more detail later in this chapter.*
[2] *See Chapter 11.*

Example ➤
A trader buys one million of a eurobond with an 8⅞ per cent coupon at 100⅛ per cent. There is six months' accrued interest on this bond as at the settlement date.

$$\text{Gain per day } 0.08875 \times \frac{1,000,000}{360} = 246.53$$

$$\text{Loss per day } 0.0811 \times \frac{100.125 + 4.4375^*}{360} = 235.56$$

Positive/negative carry = 10.97 positive (246.53 − 235.56)

$$[\ ^* \text{A}/\text{I} = (0.08875 \times \frac{180}{360} \times 100 = 4.4375)]$$

This example involves a straightforward borrowing of cash to pay for a purchase of bonds, although long positions in liquid, top quality securities, can also be financed via the repo market. This is discussed later.

Failing to deliver

The following example shows how much money can be lost when a trader fails to deliver a security.

Example ➤
• Friday, 8 December 1995
A trader sells short 1mm of a US dollar-denominated eurobond with a 9 per cent coupon at a price of 99 per cent, for regular settlement on Wednesday 13 December 1995. Proceeds of this transaction are:

Principal	990,000 (1mm x 99%)
280 days' accrued interest	70,000 (1mm x .09 x 280 / 360)
Total proceeds	1,060,000

• Monday, 11 December 1995
Even if the trader covers his short today, he will 'fail to deliver' for one day. This is because normal settlement is three days, and a trade done today will not settle until Thursday. The trader will therefore lose $250, being one day's accrued interest. To compensate, he must now buy his eurobonds back at 98.975 per cent. To calculate the cost of failing to deliver a security for one day, take the nominal amount x the coupon / 360, e.g. for this bond 1mm x 0.09 / 360 = 250.

• Tuesday, 12 December 1995
The market is unchanged and the trader can buy his eurobonds back at
99¹⁄₁₆ per cent but decides not to. Consequently, he will now fail over the
weekend and lose two more days' accrued interest, because his next
opportunity to trade will be on Wednesday for settlement the following
Monday. To compensate, he must now buy the eurobonds back at 98.925
per cent.

• Wednesday, 13 December 1995
Trader covers his short at 99 per cent for regular settlement on Monday 18
December. Proceeds:

Principal	990,000 (1mm x 99%)
285 days' accrued interest	71,250 (1mm x .09 x 285 / 360)
Total proceeds	1,061,250

This trader lost $1250 as a result of failing to deliver for five days.
Had he decided to pay the higher price of 99¹⁄₁₆ per cent to cover his short
on Tuesday, the proceeds would have been:

Principal	990,625 (1mm x 99¹⁄₁₆%)
282 days' accrued interest	70,500 (1mm x .09 x 282 / 360)
Total proceeds	1,061,125

Although Tuesday's offer price of 99¹⁄₁₆ per cent was higher than where the
trader originally sold bonds short, it would still have been cheaper overall
to buy the bonds back then, at that price, as this would have prevented a
fail over a weekend.

When a trader fails to deliver a bond, he loses the coupon interest per
day, multiplied by the number of days the bond is not delivered. As the
majority of transactions are settled on a 'delivery versus payment' basis,
when a trader fails to deliver a security, he cannot gain access to the sale
proceeds and, as a result, he also loses the financing rate on that money, as
you will see further on.

The moral of the story is that unless you are confident of being able to buy
bonds back at a cheaper price than where you short them, a price that fully
reflects the costs of being short in addition to some principal gain, do not
go short. Also, bear in mind that a security may be trading very
expensively for the very reason that there are no bonds available either to
buy or to borrow.

A fail can be avoided if bonds can be borrowed.

Borrowing securities

Euroclear and Cedel are the two largest clearing agents for international securities. The majority of transactions are settled via these organizations and both operate securities' borrowing and lending schemes.

By lending out securities, you can earn additional income without any additional market risk. By borrowing securities, whilst you will pay a borrowing fee, you can reduce your overall costs of being short.

Never assume, however, that you can borrow bonds. Always ask your finance division/settlements department, whether a security is available (for borrowing) before you go short.

Borrowing costs are calculated on the market value of a security, plus accrued interest—not the redemption amount. If a coupon payment date falls while a security is out on loan, the borrower of the securities must immediately make the appropriate coupon payment to the lender.

In the previous example, had the trader been able to borrow the eurobonds at a rate of say, 3½ per cent the first day that he went short, although he would have paid $515.27 borrowing costs (3½ per cent for five days on principal + A/I of $1,060,000) he would at least have had access to the sale proceeds of $1,060,000. His borrowing requirements for overnight funds would have then been reduced by this amount, thereby saving one day's interest at the financing rate. Alternatively, he could have used the sale proceeds to buy other securities on which coupon interest could have been earned.

The borrowing and lending of securities is a highly-lucrative, low-risk activity. A lot of money can be made from acting as the intermediary between borrowers and lenders. This is why many of the larger Street firms now operate their own schemes, as well as trade short and long positions via the repo market.

The repo market

The repo market offers an alternative way to borrow and lend both securities and cash. The repo market in Europe grew in the late 1980s in an effort to reduce what was regarded as the exorbitant cost of borrowing securities through the clearing agents. A few firms starting borrowing and lending among themselves, via the sale and repurchase of securities (repo agreements), and their purchase and re-sale (reverse repo agreements). A repo is therefore a way to lend bonds and borrow money, while a reverse repo is a way to borrow bonds and lend money.

The majority of repo trading takes place in government securities. Repos in international securities (eurobonds and global bonds) account for about

10 per cent of the turnover. This is because most government markets are much bigger and therefore more liquid.

The following is an example involving 10 million of the current US Government long bond which, at the time of writing, is the 7⅝% 15 February 2025, currently trading at a price of 111⁸⁄₃₂ per cent, i.e. 111.25.

Example ➤

You lend (repo) 10 million of this security to another party (which could be another professional or a client institution) for one week at a repo rate of 5.6 per cent. Repo interest is calculated actual/360 on the full price, i.e. the quoted net price plus accrued interest.

Interest on US Treasuries is paid on an actual/actual semi-annual basis. The number of days in a semi-annual period can vary between 181 and 184.

There are 181 days in the current interest period, and 154 days' accrued interest as of the start date (the initial settlement date) of the agreement.

On the initial settlement, or start date of the agreement, you (the lender of the securities) will receive proceeds of US$11,449,378.45:

Principal	11, 125,000.00
+ 154 days A/I	324,378.45 (10,000,000 x 0.038125 / 181 x 154)
Total proceeds	11, 449,378.45

There will be repo interest of US$12,467.10 due on this transaction (11,449,378.45 x 0.056 x 7 / 360 = 12,467.10). At the end of the agreement therefore, when you repurchase the securities, you will pay 11,461,845.55 (11,449,378.45 + 12,467.10).

A repo agreement contains an agreement by the buyer (borrower) of securities to waive all rights to any coupon payment in favour of the seller (lender) of the securities. Thus, when a coupon payment occurs part-way through a repo agreement, it has the effect of leaving the buyer (borrower) under-collateralized. This is because he would originally have loaned the seller (lender) an amount of money equal to the market price of the security, plus accrued interest. This problem is usually solved by the seller (lender) repaying the buyer (borrower) the accrued interest portion of the funds advanced at the beginning of the agreement. This is effected through what is known in the trade as a *call for difference*. Such requests come from the buyer (borrower) and are usually made in sufficient time for funds to be repaid when the seller (lender) receives the coupon payment.

In the earlier example, you borrowed money and pledged securities as collateral, and paid interest of 5.6 per cent. Thus, you could have purchased these securities and then lent them out on repo, using the resulting money borrowed to pay for them. This is how many traders finance their inventory. Whereas in the first example on financing long positions, we said the trader gains the coupon income, but loses the financing rate multiplied by the amount borrowed, if he uses the repo market, he gains the coupon income—but loses the repo rate multiplied by the amount borrowed.

It is important to remember, however, that the quality of collateral will determine the repo rate. In this example, we used US government securities, which represent the highest quality collateral. If you wanted to repo out one million of a eurobond issued by a bank or corporate borrower, it could be difficult given the credit and liquidity risk and small amount involved. These risks would be reflected in the repo rate; you may have to pledge more collateral and/or pay a much higher rate. When financing long eurobond positions therefore, the traditional approach may prove the cheapest.

Financing short positions

On short eurobond positions where bonds are available for borrow, the trader:

LOSES coupon income x par amount
LOSES borrowing costs x amount borrowed (principal + A/I)
GAINS financing rate x proceeds (from short sale)

Example ➤

A trader sells short one million of a eurobond with an $8\frac{3}{4}$ per cent coupon at a price of 101 per cent. There is 314 days' accrued interest on this bond as at the settlement date. The borrowing rate, i.e. the cost of borrowing bonds from Euroclear or Cedel, is $3\frac{1}{2}$ per cent.

Loss per day: 0.0875 x 1mm / 360	= 243.05 Loss
Loss per day: 0.035 x 1,086,319.44* / 360	= 105.61 Loss
Gain per day: 0.0811 x 1,086,319.44 / 360	= 244.72 Gain
Positive/negative carry	103.94 Negative

$*\begin{cases} \textit{Principal} & 1,010,000.00 \\ \textit{314 days'}\ \text{A/I} & 76,319.44 \\ \hline & 1,086,319.44 \end{cases}$

As with long positions, a trader can also finance short positions in the repo market by borrowing bonds via a *reverse repo* agreement. He would use the bonds he borrows to make delivery on his short sale, and lend (pledge) the resulting proceeds of his short sale to the repo desk as collateral. He would then receive interest income from the repo desk, on the money pledged as collateral. If, therefore, the reverse repo rate was 6 per cent the trader would:

LOSE coupon income x par amount (on his short sale)
GAIN reverse repo rate x amount loaned (principal + A/I from short sale)

Going back to the last example, while the trader would still lose 243.05 per day in coupon income, he would gain 181.05 from his reverse repo (0.06 x 1,086,319.44 / 360 = 181.05) resulting in a net loss per day of 62 instead of 103.94.

Therefore, when financing short positions via the repo market, the trader's net loss or gain is the difference between the coupon on the bond he sells short, and the reverse repo rate. His net loss or gain on long positions, is the difference between the coupon on the bond he owns, and the repo rate.

Although in the US government bond example a period of one week is used, repos are often done for just a few days, and trades involving 50 or 100 million bonds and more, are quite common. In fact, a key advantage of the repo market is that bonds can be borrowed for a fixed period, and there is no limit on transaction size. Euroclear and Cedel only lend or borrow on an overnight basis, and also limit the lending of securities to 10 per cent of an issue, regardless of whether there are holders willing to lend more. They impose this restriction as their priority is to help create liquidity rather than restrict it, which could occur if one party controlled too many bonds of one issue.

Repos and reverse repos in effect, resemble collateralized loans. Investors can earn additional income from lending (repo-ing) securities held in their portfolio, while organizations with surplus cash can lend these funds on a collateralized basis using a reverse repo.

Tri-party repo agreements

Tri-party repos provide another way for Street firms to borrow money to finance their inventories, and a way for organizations to lend money safely. It also enables organizations with a lot of money, but inadequate clearance systems and/or an insufficient number of settlements staff, to participate in the market.

The first tri-party repo agreement in Europe was executed in October 1992 between the EBRD, Swiss Bank Corporation, and Cedel.

The concept originated in the US but many adaptations were required for the non-US government and international markets, given the different currencies, settlement procedures, and associated legal considerations.

The tri-party repo structure involves a third-party acting as clearing agent and custodian, as well as a sort of policeman. At the present time Cedel, Euroclear or the Bank of New York can act as tri-party custodians.

The custodian's role is to clear all transactions, monitor and control the quantity and quality of collateral, and ensure that all margin calls are met. If, therefore, 100 million Bunds (German government bonds) are on repo at a market price of 100 per cent, but then the market falls by, say, two points, the custodian is responsible for ensuring that additional securities are pledged. This is to ensure that the organization which has borrowed those bonds has collateral equal to the market price paid at the start of the agreement. In the same way, when securities pledged as collateral are downgraded, the custodian is responsible for ensuring that securities of acceptable quality are immediately substituted. The level of collateralization required is not always 100 per cent. Some central banks for example, require 101 per cent, which means they will lend DM100,000,000 but will want securities as collateral that are worth DM101,000,000.

The tri-party repo structure allows for unlimited right of substitution. In both of the above situations, therefore, different securities could be used either as a substitute or to make up any shortfall. A dealer that pledges securities under a tri-party structure, can therefore actively trade them, knowing that if he sells the securities, and needs them to make good delivery, he can simply substitute.

Custodian's fees are paid by the trading house, and reflected in the trader's quoted rate, which must still, of course, be competitive to attract the business.

Tri-party repos provide the Street with access to pools of money they may not otherwise be able to borrow directly. Their structure enables organizations to participate in the repo market safely, and with minimum administrative hassle.

Matched-book trading

A finance department that has good repo traders, can generate significant revenue from actively trading the repo market via what they call their *matched book*. Matched-book trading is a bit of a misnomer, in that it involves anticipating which securities and currencies will be in demand, and taking positions accordingly. Profits come from accurately predicting the direction of interest rates in various currencies and the supply of, and demand for, specific securities.

For example, when a government trader goes short, he will usually look to borrow bonds from his repo desk which, if running a matched book, may already have some in position. If the repo desk accurately predicted that the security in question would be in short supply, then they will have borrowed bonds ahead of time.

Some firms have computer programs which measure the probability of fails in different securities. If the repo trader has bonds in position, he will lend them to the government trader at the prevailing repo rate, thereby earning the difference between his initial cost and the repo rate. If the repo trader does not run a matched book, or does not have the security in position, he would have to go into the market to borrow it at that time. However, if the government trader was taken short because he quoted a price, and someone bought bonds on his offer and he did not therefore choose to be short, the security could well be unavailable for borrowing. Matched-book trading can provide considerable additional liquidity to a firm's trading divisions.

Finance activities have become very sophisticated, and finance desks are increasingly being measured like any other trading desk (except of course, that profit is a function of money saved as well as money earned). This is not to say that individual trading divisions are treated as clients of the finance division when borrowing money to finance their inventories. Money borrowed to finance in-house trading activities may be passed to the relevant trading divisions at cost, with each division paying a portion of the finance desk's operating costs. You should find out how your firm works in this regard.

Houses with the highest credit-rating, and the most capital, are in the best position to develop sophisticated repo operations. Banks and other financial institutions will extend credit to them at the lowest rates, and investors will be happy to lend their securities to them. By the same token, to ensure their standing is maintained, any firm active in the repo market must be extremely thorough when assessing the creditworthiness of all counterparties with whom it deals. It must also have strict criteria for assessing the quality and value of collateral and, given the sheer volumes and short-term nature of repo agreements, first-class technological support to both settle trades, and monitor accurately the inherent risks.

Value date mistakes

Settlement procedures vary between markets. It is therefore essential to confirm the value (settlement) date of a trade at the time of execution, so as to ensure that it is a 'good business day' according to the prescribed criteria. A seemingly trivial mistake can cost a lot of money and administrative hassle. For more than 30 years, normal/regular settlement of international securities was seven calendar days. On 1 June 1995, it changed to three business days following the trade date, providing that both clearing agents are open for business (Euroclear and Cedel usually open all year round except for Christmas Day). Additionally, the cash market for the underlying currency in which transfers are to be made, must also be open for business.

This change reduces risk, in that the less time between trade date and settlement date, the less likely a counterparty could go bankrupt in the interim. It also brings the eurobond markets more in line with the foreign exchange and government markets, where settlement usually takes place one or two days following trade date. It is now easier for investors to switch between eurobonds and government securities denominated in different currencies.

That said, a seemingly inconsequential oversight with regard to settlement details can impact on a series of transactions, which can cost money, and adversely affect relationships. Clients, in particular, do not like settlement mistakes. For example, let us say that you are a client and sell a eurobond on a Monday for normal settlement the following Thursday, three days later. You then find out, after the trade is done, that the Thursday is a holiday in the US (where the cash market for US dollars is based). In this situation you would not receive the proceeds of your sale until the Friday. Although there would be an adjustment of accrued interest, problems can still arise. What if, for example, having traded on the assumption that your sale would settle on the Thursday, you had entered into a foreign exchange agreement to convert your US dollar proceeds into French francs in order to pay for a purchase of French franc government bonds due to settle on the same day?

Time spent unravelling a settlements error is time that could be spent making money. Misunderstandings about value dates can easily occur. Always confirm the value date of a transaction at the time of execution.

Positive fails

As the average size of a eurobond issue is much greater now than it was ten years ago, you would have to have the capacity to buy and own a lot of bonds to successfully create a 'positive fail'. Your firm's capital and your time, could perhaps be better used elsewhere. However, the economic rewards of positive fails can be considerable and so they do still occur.

Creating a positive fail involves picking a security in which there is little supply, buying sufficient amounts of it so as to take the market short, and then refusing to lend out your bonds.

In this situation, the trader would earn the coupon, and use of the money to be set aside to pay for the bonds, which will sit in his account until bonds are delivered. He could then use this money to reduce his overnight cash borrowings and therefore his financing costs.

A positive fail can be left to run for as long as the trader wants. Unless short-sellers manage to find bonds to deliver, they are at the trader's mercy. If and when he decides to end their misery, he could make even more money by offering bonds back to them at a very high price. If their only alternative is to continue failing, they have little choice but to pay up.

In the repo market, a bond that is trading expensively because it is scarce and unavailable for borrow, is known as a *special*. A repo trader could therefore work in conjunction with his eurobond traders to create specials.

Positive fails can generate a lot of revenue. Be alert to the possibility that you could find yourself caught in one if you fail in your due diligence as a trader.[1] In fact, in the 1980s, some firms indulged in the practice of selling short new issues in which they had no known sources of supply. Some positive fails were thus created and a few firms lost a small fortune.

Avoiding fails on sales

Other than when buying and selling identical amounts[2] when you sell a large amount of one particular bond, it is prudent to split the ticket. If you sell 20 million bonds to the same institution, split the ticket into four separate trades of five million. If you request this at the time of execution, your counterparty should be happy to oblige. If they are not, then ask yourself why. Even if you own a lot of bonds, unless you are certain that all bonds purchased have been delivered, a fail could occur if the securities are sold in one piece.

Example ➤
A trader buys 5mm of a bond on a Monday, from three different sources: two lots of 2mm and one lot of 1mm. He then sells all 5mm in one piece. He then finds that, of the 5mm bonds purchased, only 2mm have been received. His buyer's delivery instructions however, are to receive one piece of 5mm. This trade will not settle unless the buyer accepts a partial

---

[1] *See 'Trading' in Chapter 6.*

[2] *When buying and selling identical amounts, it could have the effect of 'zero' on your credit line if transactions are 'netted' out. If this is the case, were you to buy 50 million of a security, and then sell 50 million—but split the ticket into five lots of 10 million, the trade will not be netted out. This is to your disadvantage as it will use up 50 million of your credit line. If you have a limited credit line, and are running big overall positions, do not split tickets. Try instead to match purchase and sale amounts wherever possible.*

delivery, which is unlikely for reasons explained below. The seller will, therefore, fail on the whole amount.

A buyer of a block of bonds is in effect provided with free financing if he refuses to accept a partial delivery. If the seller cannot deliver all the bonds, the buyer does not have to pay for them. This money will therefore remain in the buyer's account until such time as all the bonds are delivered. While it cannot be removed, it can be used to reduce overnight borrowings, on which interest would have to be paid at the financing rate.

Conversely and consequently, the seller will have to finance any partial amount of securities in his account, but will not earn the coupon, as it belongs to the buyer from the settlement date. Unless the partial amount was sufficiently large and of good credit quality, it is unlikely the seller could even repo the bonds out on an overnight basis to reduce financing costs. When selling a large amount of bonds, you should therefore split the tickets.

Chapter 14

138

GLOSSARY FOR CHAPTER 14

Reuters *Abacus*
A computer program designed and owned by Reuters that identifies anomalies in the foreign exchange market and thereby opportunities for arbitrage.

spot
Originated from *on the spot,* meaning to deal now for the most immediate settlement possible, which is usually the day following a transaction.

volatility
A measurement of the price movement of a security during a specific period.

Chapter 14

Introduction to foreign exchange

A lthough this book is essentially a bond book, the following brief introduction to foreign exchange (FX) is necessary, given the FX market's influence on the bond markets.

The foreign exchange market is the market where currencies are bought and sold. Of the US$1 trillion(!) traded daily, approximately 98 per cent is for non-trade purposes. This is the result of the development of swap markets, deregulation, and the diversification of the portfolios of many investors.

How currency and exchange rates are defined

Exchange rates are quantified in units of one currency versus another. Generally, the currency denominated in larger units is expressed in units of the smaller, e.g.:

Deutschemarks per US dollar
Italian lire per Deutschemark

Two rules of thumb:

1. Most US dollar rates are defined in terms of other currencies
2. Most sterling rates are defined in terms of other currencies

All currencies are relative. A currency cannot rise in isolation! Thus, at any given time, a currency can rise against one currency, but fall against another.

Cross exchange rates

From a list of simple exchange rates you can calculate cross rates.

$$\frac{\text{Deutschemark}}{\text{US dollar}} \times \frac{\text{US dollar}}{\text{sterling}} = \frac{\text{Deutschemark}}{\text{sterling}}$$

Characteristics of a foreign-exchange transaction

A spot foreign exchange contract is an agreement between two counterparties to exchange an agreed amount of one currency for another currency at an agreed rate. Settlement is typically two working days after the transaction.

In a transaction, the market often omits the 'big figure' e.g. $1.6320-30 may be read out as '20-30'. It is *critical*, therefore, to make sure that you repeat all details back at the time of execution so as to ensure that you have the correct 'handle', i.e. the big figure!

An *open* position exists where, due to being net long/short of currencies, there is an exposure to FX risk. If there is no open position, then it is *square*.

Spot and forward transactions

The forward foreign-exchange market offers protection against a future foreign-exchange risk. Forward rates of exchange are determined by interest-rate differentials between currencies. The forward rate is an adjustment to compensate the holder of a lower-yielding currency until conversion into that with a higher yield.

If the sterling-dollar rate was 1.50, with sterling rates at 6 per cent and US rates at five per cent, 1,000,000 would, at the end of one year, produce £1,060,000 or US$1,575,000. The assumption with the latter, is that you would convert sterling to dollars today and then reinvest for one year at five per cent. But if you ultimately wanted US$ in one year's time, you would want to know the sterling-dollar rate, one year forward.

In order to calculate the forward rate, work out the rate that would compensate the holder of dollars for the period concerned. The rate is that which equalizes two sums at the end of one year.

If the rate is fixed at $(1,575,000/1,060,000) = $1.4858, then the sums are equalized in dollar terms. This implies that expectations are for sterling to be weaker by 1.42 cents. This is known as the currency's *discount* to the dollar. Conversely, the dollar is at a *premium* to sterling.

The forward exchange rate is only an identity linking interest rate differentials and currency rates.

Example ➤

US$/£

	Forward rate
Spot 1.4750 - 1.4760	-
1-month 0.0016 - 0.0014	= 1.4734 - 1.4746
3-month 0.0047 - 0.0044	= 1.4703 - 1.4716

Double check! The bid must always be lower than the offer. If it is not, then you have subtracted instead of added (or vice versa)!

If you want to buy dollars versus selling sterling in one months' time, the two main alternatives are to buy dollars forward, or buy dollars spot and deposit the proceeds for one month until required. The latter is called a *swap transaction*, and the calculations are similar, as can be shown by the following:

Example ➤
If 1,000,000 is the amount to be converted to dollars in one month's time, and the one-month sterling interest rate is 5 per cent, while the one-month dollar interest rate is 3¾ per cent, the choices are:

1) To invest 1,000,000, and earn one month's interest of 4,166.67, giving a total value of 1,004,166.67, and then convert to dollars at the forward rate of 1.4734,

   or,

2) To sell sterling for dollars today which would provide $1,475,000, and earn one month's interest of $4,609.37, giving a total value of $1,479,609.37. This would translate into an effective exchange rate on the swap of 1.4735 (1,479,609.37/1,004,166.67 = 1.4735).

Via the forward transaction, which would be simpler since it only involves one trade, it would be possible to sell sterling for dollars at a rate of 1.4734 = $1,473,400.

This example makes the forward transaction unattractive whereas, in reality, there is usually very little difference since FX dealers are adept at identifying anomalies—and taking advantage of them within seconds. There are various mechanisms for identifying such opportunities, such as the Reuters *Abacus* system. Treasury managers who regularly hedge multi-currency positions invariably look for the cheapest hedge, as the savings can be substantial over the course of a year.

Although, occasionally, the more complex and/or administratively cumbersome transaction may be cheaper, where there appears to be a saving, do factor in any additional administrative time and hassle. Remember, too, that a dealer's spreads are influenced by the volatility of the market, and liquidity of the various currencies traded (including time of day, exchange controls, transaction size).

Factors influencing the foreign-exchange market

As the exchange rate between two currencies is a relative price, the factors which move the exchange rate are dependent on the relative performance of one economy against the other, relative political developments, and differences in supply and demand. Influences can be of three types:

- Economic
- Political
- Psychological

The main economic factors are:

- Relative interest rates
- Relative inflation rates
- Performance of the balance of payments
- Government policy

Political influences can be both domestic and international. Psychological influences reflect market expectations, and are generally short-term in nature, and often assessed by means of *technical* or *chart* analysis. Such analysis may identify particular important psychological levels for a market.

Chapter 15

Chapter 15

Bond mathematics

To reiterate what was stated in Chapter 3, the mathematical sections in this book do not aim to examine the merits of one concept over another. Rather, they aim to show how to do the calculations that have become market convention.

A bond's yield-to-maturity, commonly known as *YTM* or simply just *yield*, is based on its coupon, maturity and price. It is what an investor will earn from an asset each year, expressed as an interest rate. A 5-year bond with a 9 per cent coupon and a redemption price of 100 per cent will yield more than 9 per cent if purchased at a price of 99 per cent, and less than 9 per cent if purchased at a price of 101 per cent.

Most bond mathematics involve the manipulation of present and future values and their implied interest rates, and consists of multiplication, division, addition and subtraction. The key to finding the correct solution is to do the actions in the right sequence. This is very important. Since all bond mathematics essentially breaks down into a series of future and present cashflows, this is a logical place to start.

Calculating future values

If you take $1.00 today and invest it for three years at an annual rate of interest of 10 per cent, by the end of the third year your $1 will increase in value to $1.3310 by the following formula:

$$(1+.10)^3 = 1.3310$$

at the end of year 1, $1.00 will grow to $1.10
at the end of year 2, $1.00 will grow to $1.210 (1.10 x 1.10)
at the end of year 3, $1.00 will grow to $1.3310 (1.10 x 1.10 x 1.10)

As you can see the above is simply a series of multiplications and the formula is therefore:

$$(1+r)^n$$

where,

r   interest rate expressed as a decimal

n   number of times compounding occurs during investment period.

To calculate the future value of a present sum of money that is compounded on a semi-annual basis, the formula becomes:

$$(1 + \frac{r}{f})^n$$

where,

f   compounding frequency per year

Therefore, to find the future value of $1.00 compounded semi-annually at 10 per cent for three years, the equation is $(1 + \frac{.10}{2})^6$, calculated as follows:

    1.05 x 1.05 x 1.05 x 1.05 x 1.05 x 1.05 = 1.3401

Calculating present values

The calculation of a present value amount is simply the reciprocal of the future value formula:

$$\frac{1}{(1 + r)^n} \quad \text{or} \quad \frac{1}{(1 + \frac{r}{f})^n}$$

Therefore, finding the present value of a sum of money that—in three years—will amount to $1.3310, assuming an annual rate of interest of 10 per cent, involves a series of divisions as follows:

    $1.3310 / 1.10 / 1.10 / 1.10 / = $1.00

The answer must be $1.00 as it must mirror the future value calculation.

To find out how much money you would need today to generate $1.50 in two years' time, assuming interest of 10 per cent payable quarterly, the equation becomes:

$$\frac{1.50}{(1 + \frac{.10}{4})^8}$$

$n = 8$ (2 yrs x 4 periods per year) and $r = 0.025$ (10% ÷ 4 quarterly periods)

$$\frac{1.50}{1.025^8} = \$1.2311$$

Conversely, the future value of $1.2311 compounded quarterly for two years is $1.50.

To recap, to find the future value of an amount multiply by one plus the interest rate (compound). To find the present value, divide by one plus the interest rate (discount).

Zero-coupon bonds: Finding the price, given the yield

As their name suggests, zero-coupon bonds do not pay interest during their life. Instead, the interest is all rolled into one and paid out at maturity. Therefore, to work out the price for a given yield on a zero-coupon bond, simply use the present value formula:

$$\frac{1}{(1+r)^n} \quad \text{or} \quad \frac{1}{(1+\frac{r}{f})^n}$$

Figure 15.1 shows a price/yield chart for zero-coupon bonds with a redemption amount of par. This is a simple grid containing present value amounts. It tells you that (credit risk and technical considerations aside) the price of a 30-year zero-coupon bond, if it is to yield 9 per cent interest

	1%	2%	3%	4%	5%	6%	7%	8%	9%	10%
1 yr	99.01	98.04	97.09	96.15	95.24	94.34	93.46	92.59	91.74	90.91
2 yrs	98.03	96.12	94.26	92.46	90.70	89.00	87.34	85.73	84.17	82.64
3 yrs	97.06	94.23	91.51	88.90	86.38	83.96	81.63	79.38	77.22	75.13
5 yrs	95.15	90.57	86.26	82.19	78.35	74.73	71.30	68.06	64.99	62.09
7 yrs	93.27	87.06	81.31	75.99	71.07	66.51	62.27	58.35	54.70	51.32
10 yrs	90.53	82.03	74.41	67.56	61.39	55.84	50.83	46.32	42.24	38.55
20 yrs	81.95	67.30	55.37	45.64	37.69	31.18	25.84	21.45	17.84	14.86
30 yrs	74.19	55.21	41.20	30.83	23.14	17.41	13.14	9.94	7.54	5.73

	11%	12%	13%	14%	15%	16%	17%	18%	19%	20%
1 yr	90.09	89.29	88.50	87.72	86.96	86.21	85.47	84.75	84.03	83.33
2 yrs	81.16	79.72	78.31	76.95	75.61	74.32	73.05	71.82	70.62	69.44
3 yrs	73.12	71.18	69.31	67.50	65.75	64.07	62.44	60.86	59.34	57.87
5 yrs	59.35	56.74	54.28	51.94	49.72	47.61	45.61	43.71	41.90	40.19
7 yrs	48.17	45.23	42.51	39.96	37.59	35.38	33.32	31.39	29.59	27.91
10 yrs	35.22	32.20	29.46	26.97	24.72	22.67	20.80	19.11	17.56	16.15
20 yrs	12.40	10.37	8.68	7.28	6.11	5.14	4.33	3.65	3.08	2.61
30 yrs	4.37	3.34	2.56	1.96	1.51	1.16	0.90	0.70	0.54	0.42

Figure 15.1   Price/yield chart for zero-coupon bonds (redemption amount = 100)

148

annually, should be 7.54 per cent whereas, at a yield of 10 per cent, it should be 5.73 per cent.

This grid is also useful for approximating prices and yields which fall between the given ranges. For example, a 10-year zero, to yield 9½ per cent, will cost about 40.39 per cent which is the average of 42.24 per cent (the price at a yield of 9 per cent) and 38.55 per cent (the price at a yield of 10 per cent). At a yield of 9½ per cent, the precise price is 40.35 per cent.

Coupon bonds: Finding the price, given the yield

To calculate a price, it is necessary to know the coupon, frequency of coupon payments, maturity and yield of the bond. To find a price for a given yield on a eurobond, discount future coupon (interest) payments and principal to their present values, add these amounts together and then deduct accrued interest.

Example ➤
There is a eurobond that matures in one year and pays an annual coupon of 10 per cent. Yields for periods of one-year are about 6⅞ per cent on an actual/360 basis. As eurobonds pay interest on a 30/360 basis this bond would be an attractive investment at a yield of 7 per cent. You therefore want to calculate the correct price for a yield of 7 per cent. The price at this yield is 102.80 per cent.

$$P = \frac{10}{(1+.07)^1} + \frac{100}{(1+.07)^1}$$

$$9.346 \quad + \quad 93.458 = 102.80\%$$

The formula for this calculation is:

$$p = \frac{CPN_1}{(1+r)^1} + \frac{CPN_2}{(1+r)^2} + \frac{CPN_n}{(1+r)^n} + \frac{PRINC_n}{(1+r)^n}$$

where,

p price of the bond
CPN coupon flows from the bond in periods 1, 2, ...n. i.e. a 2-year annual pay bond has two coupon payments whereas a 2-year semi-annual bond has 4.
$PRINC$ principal from bond in period n (maturity)
r discount rate (bond's yield-to-maturity)
n compounding periods, i.e. a 2-yr annual pay bond has two compounding periods, whereas a 2-yr semi-annual bond has 4.

Example ➤
The price for a yield of 7 per cent on a 10 per cent annual pay 3-year eurobond, is 107.87 per cent calculated as follows:

$$P = \frac{10}{(1.07)^1} + \frac{10}{(1.07)^2} + \frac{110}{(1.07)^3}$$

$$9.346 \qquad 8.734 \qquad 89.793 \;=\; 107.87\%$$

Coupon bonds: Finding the price, given the yield on a bond that is trading with accrued interest

The following example shows how to find the price at a yield of 7 per cent on a eurobond with a 10 per cent coupon maturing in two years and 267 days, i.e. a bond where the initial compounding period is less than one.

Example ➤
The first whole compounding period for this bond begins in 267 days and ends one year later. Thus after one year and 267 days you will receive a 10 per cent coupon, and after two years and 267 days, 110 per cent (a 10 per cent coupon plus 100 per cent principal repayment as this is when the bond will mature). Discounting these cashflows for one and two years respectively will determine their values 267 days from settlement. We will deal with the coupon payment due in 267 days at the end, as it makes the arithmetic simpler:

$$P = \frac{10}{(1.07)^1} + \frac{110}{(91.07)^2}$$

$$9.346 \qquad 96.078 \;=\; 105.424\%$$

Now add the coupon payment of 10 which is due in 267 days, making a sum total of 115.424, which could be viewed as the present value for this bond in 267 days.

You must now discount this amount to its present value using the 267-day rate, i.e. the rate that reflects the partial period. The calculation for finding this rate is as follows:[1]

$$(1 + 0.07)^{267/360} = 1.0515$$

---

[1] *1 + (0.07 x 267/360) will produce an approximate rate. This approach, while rough, is often used by the market.*

Thus, 115.424 must now be discounted by this rate.

115.424 / 1.0515 = 109.77

This is the 'full price' for this bond, in that it includes 2.583 accrued interest (93 days at 10 per cent; 100 x 0.10 x 93/360), which must be deducted. 109.77 minus 2.583 = 107.19. The correct price for this bond for a yield of 7 per cent is therefore 107.19 per cent.

Discount securities: Finding the price given the discount rate

An example of how to convert a discount rate into an equivalent yield can be found in Chapter 11. In addition, it is useful to know what a discount rate equates to in terms of price as investment decisions can be a function of how much money a client has to spend. The formula for finding the price for a given discount rate, is as follows:

$$P = F(1 - \frac{dt}{360})$$

where,

P	price
F	face value of discount security
d	discount rate (as a decimal)
t	days from settlement to maturity

Therefore, a discount security with 91 days remaining from settlement until maturity, trading at 6.10 per cent, with a redemption value of $100, will cost $98.46.

$$\text{Price} = \$100\,(1 - 0.061 \times \frac{91}{360}) = \$100\,(0.98458) = \$98.46$$

Figure 15.2 provides a desktop summary which can be useful in your daily work. It may help to keep it close by at all times!

MODIFIED DURATION GRID
Yield change for price change of 1 per cent on bonds trading at, or close to, par

	3%	4%	5%	6%	7%	8%	9%	10%	11%	12%	13%	14%	15%	20%
3yrs	36	36	37	38	38	39	40	40	41	42	43	43	44	48
5yrs	22	23	23	24	25	25	26	27	27	28	29	29	30	34
7yrs	16	17	17	18	19	19	20	21	21	22	23	23	24	28
10yrs	12	12	13	14	14	15	16	16	17	18	19	19	20	24
20yrs	7	7	8	9	10	10	11	12	13	14	14	15	16	21
30yrs	5	6	7	7	8	9	10	11	12	13	13	14	15	20
40yrs	4	5	6	7	8	8	9	10	11	12	13	14	15	20
50yrs	4	5	6	6	7	8	9	10	11	12	13	14	15	20

CONVERSION OF SEMI-ANNUAL AND ANNUAL YIELDS.

Annual to semi-annual			Semi-annual to annual		
annual	semi-annual	differential	semi-annual	annual	differential
2%	1.99%	1	2%	2.01%	1
3%	2.98%	2	3%	3.02%	2
4%	3.96%	4	4%	4.04%	4
5%	4.94%	6	5%	5.08%	6
6%	5.91%	9	6%	6.09%	9
7%	6.88%	12	7%	7.12%	12
8%	7.85%	15	8%	8.16%	16
9%	8.81%	19	9%	9.20%	20
10%	9.76%	24	10%	10.25%	25
11%	10.71%	29	11%	11.30%	30
12%	11.66%	34	12%	12.36%	36
13%	12.60%	40	13%	13.42%	42
14%	13.54%	46	14%	14.49%	49
15%	14.48%	52	15%	15.56%	56
20%	19.09%	91	20%	21.00%	100

DECIMAL/FRACTION EQUIVALENTS
and value per mm

						USD VALUE OF 0.01%/MM	
1/32	0.03125	312.50	9/16	0.56250	5625.00	1 day	$0.28
1/16	0.06250	625.00	5/8	0.62500	6250.00	30 days	$8.33
1/8	0.12500	1250.00	11/16	0.68750	6875.00	60 days	$16.67
3/16	0.18750	1875.00	3/4	0.75000	7500.00	90 days	$25.00
1/4	0.25000	2500.00	13/16	0.81250	8125.00	180 days	$50.00
5/16	0.31250	3125.00	7/8	0.87500	9750.00	270 days	$75.00
3/8	0.37500	3750.00	15/16	0.93750	9375.00	360 days	$100.00
7/16	0.43750	4375.00	1	1.00000	10,000.00		
1/2	0.50000	5000.00					

Figure 15.2   Desktop summary of trading grids

Chapter 16

Chapter 16

Modified duration

There are two main types of duration. Never confuse the two. You cannot hedge positions using Macaulay's duration,[1] whereas hedging is possible using 'modified duration'. Traders are therefore more concerned with modified duration. All further references to duration in this chapter are to modified duration.

Modified duration =   percentage price volatility of the full price (i.e. principal plus accrued interest) of a bond.

A bond's maturity says very little about its price sensitivity to interest rate movements. The prices of bonds of equal maturity, but different coupons, change at different rates for the same change in yield. For example, if you own two 10-year bonds, one with a 2 per cent coupon and one with a 15 per cent coupon, and yields move by 50bp (50 basis points), the change in the full price of each security will be different. Modified duration enables you to establish what the respective price movements will be, as it takes into consideration the size and frequency of all the cashflows. In the gilt market, duration is also known as volatility.

A duration of five on a coupon bond means that the full price of the security will move by 5 per cent for a 1 per cent change in yield, or by 0.05 per cent for a 1bp change in yield (100bp = 1 per cent). If the modified duration of a portfolio of bonds is 7.2 then if yields move by 1 per cent the full price of the portfolio will change by 7.2 per cent. If yields move by 50bp then the full price will change by 3.6 per cent. If yields move by just one basis point then the full price will change by 0.072 per cent.

As coupons are paid, time elapses and interest rates change, so the duration of a bond (or a portfolio of bonds) will also change. This is why it

---

[1] *Macaulay's duration was invented by Fred Macaulay in 1938 as a way of measuring the life of a coupon bond. The life of a zero-coupon bond is pure, as there are no cashflows to take into account, but the life of a coupon bond is not. Macaulay's duration measures the life of a coupon bond using a zero-coupon bond equivalent term to maturity. The formula is the same as for modified, minus the last step. It could be said therefore, that Macaulay's duration was 'modified' to be of more use. You cannot find price change for yield change, or hedge transactions using Macaulay's duration.*

is necessary to constantly re-calculate the duration of a security or an entire portfolio.

Formula for calculating modified duration

$$MD = \sum \left[\frac{[CPN_1/(1+r)^1]\,1}{p} + \frac{[CPNn/(1+r)^n]\,n}{p} + ..\frac{[PRINC^a\,p/(1+r)^n]\,n]}{p} \right] / (1+r)$$

where,

CPN	coupon payments
r	yield-to-maturity
p	price (to include accrued interest)
n	time, in years, to receipt of cashflow
PRINC	principal repayment at maturity

Note: Where coupon payments occur more than once per year, e.g. semi or quarterly r becomes r/f, where f = coupon frequency

Example ➤
The modified duration of a eurobond with a 20 per cent coupon and three years until maturity, trading at 134.1 per cent to yield 7 per cent, would therefore be 2.42, calculated as follows:

Step One	$[20 / (1.07)^1 / 134.1]$	= 0.139
Step Two	$[20 / (1.07)^2 / 134.1]\,2$	= 0.261
Step Three	$[120 / (1.07)^3 / 134.1]\,3$	= 2.191
		= 2.591
Step Four	$2.591 / (1.07)$	**= MD of 2.42**

If yields change by 1 per cent the price of this security will move by 2.42 per cent. Therefore, if yields go up by, say, 15bp to 7.15 per cent, the price will go down by 0.15 per cent of 2.42 per cent of 134.1 per cent, to approximately 133.61 per cent. In fact, using the formula for finding the price of a bond given the yield, you will find that the precise price is 133.63 per cent, calculated as follows:

$$P = \frac{20}{(1.0715)^1} + \frac{20}{(1.0715)^2} + \frac{120}{(1.0715)^3}$$

$$18.67 \quad + \quad 17.42 \quad + \quad 97.54 \quad = \quad 133.63\%$$

If a 1 per cent change in yield changes the price of this security by 2.42 per cent, then its yield will change by about 41bp if the price moves by 1 per cent.

1% change in yield = 2.42% change in price

1 / 2.42% = 41bp

1% change in price = 0.41 basis point change in yield

The reciprocal of the modified duration of a bond is its approximate change in yield for a 1 per cent movement in price. More about how this can be used later.

To find the modified duration of a bond part way through an interest period, adjust the market price for accrued interest, and then proceed as above. To adjust for accrued interest, multiply the coupon by the fraction of the year and add the result to the price.

Example ➤

The modified duration of a bond with a 5 per cent coupon, 2½ years until maturity, trading at 91.33[207] to yield 9 per cent, is 2.16, calculated as follows:

5 x 0.5 years	= 2.5 (i.e. coupon multiplied by half a year)
2.5 plus 91.33	= 93.83 [207]

Now proceed as before using the full price of 93.83[207]:

Step One	$[5 / (1.09)^{0.5} / 93.83] 0.5$	= 0.025
Step Two	$[5 / (1.09)^{1.5} / 93.83] 1.5$	= 0.070
Step Three	$[105 / (1.09)^{2.5} / 93.83] 2.5$	= 2.255
		= 2.351
Step Four	2.351 / (1.09)	**= MD of 2.16**

If yields go up by 1bp, the price of this security will go down by 0.0216 per cent, and the new market price will be 91.31[05], i.e. 93.83[207] minus 0.0216 = 93.8105, less accrued interest of 2.5, = 91.31[05].

Zero-coupon bonds

The duration of a zero-coupon bond is always identical to its maturity, because there are no coupons to consider. A 3-year zero-coupon bond yields 3 per cent at a price of 91.51 per cent, and 2.99 per cent at a price is 91.54 per cent. This is a 0.03 per cent change in the full price.

The price of a 3-year zero-coupon bond yielding 10 per cent is 75.13 per cent and, at a yield of 9.99 per cent, the price is 75.15 per cent. This is also a 0.03 per cent change in the full price (75.13 x 1.0003 = 75.15).

Convexity

The first derivative of price with respect to yield is modified duration, the second derivative is *convexity*. Simply stated, convexity is the rate at which duration changes. The following factors increase convexity:

- lower coupons
- longer maturities
- lower yields

Therefore, long-term zero-coupon bonds have greater convexity than short-term high coupon bonds. This becomes significant in the weighting of hedges.

Summary

Modified duration measures price change for yield change. Traders use it to weight trades. Bonds with a high duration exhibit greater price volatility, while bonds with a low duration are less sensitive.

When bullish, therefore, buy low-coupon bonds with long durations, and sell high-coupon bonds with short durations. **When bearish**, buy high-coupon bonds with short durations, and sell low-coupon bonds with long durations.

Calculating yields without a calculator

Using the modified duration grid (see Figure 16.1), it is possible to calculate the yield of a security in seconds, without the use of a calculator!

From the grid, it will be seen that the yield of a 10 per cent coupon 3-year bond will move by 40bp if the price moves by 1 per cent. At a price of 99 per cent, therefore, the yield will be 10.40 per cent while, at a price of 101 per cent, it will be 9.60 per cent. At a price of 99½ per cent the yield will be 10.20 per cent and, at a price of 100½ per cent, it will be 9.80 per cent. To calculate these yields you only need to memorize one number in the grid.

Once you know the yield change for a 1 per cent price change, it is easy to work out yield changes for price changes of less than 1 per cent. By memorizing the number 40, you would know that a two-way market price of 98¾ - 99 per cent for a bond with a 10 per cent coupon and three years to maturity, would translate into a yield of 10.40 per cent at the offering

MODIFIED DURATION GRID

Yield change for price change of 1 per cent on bonds trading at, or close to, par

	3%	4%	5%	6%	7%	8%	9%	10%	11%	12%	13%	14%	15%	20%
3yrs	36	36	37	38	38	39	40	40	41	42	43	43	44	48
5yrs	22	23	23	24	25	25	26	27	27	28	29	29	30	34
7yrs	16	17	17	18	19	19	20	21	21	22	23	23	24	28
10yrs	12	12	13	14	14	15	16	16	17	18	19	19	20	24
20yrs	7	7	8	9	10	10	11	12	13	14	14	15	16	21
30yrs	5	6	7	7	8	9	10	11	12	13	13	14	15	20
40yrs	4	5	6	7	8	8	9	10	11	12	13	14	15	20
50yrs	4	5	6	6	7	8	9	10	11	12	13	14	15	20

Figure 16.1   Modified duration grid

price of 99 per cent, and a yield of 10.50 per cent at the bid price of 98¾ per cent.

From the grid, you can see that a 1 per cent price move on an 8 per cent 5-year bond trading at, or close to, par is equal to 25bp. Therefore, a price move of ½ of 1 per cent will change the yield by 12½bp, while a move of ⅛ per cent will change the yield by just over three basis points.

It is not necessary to memorize all the numbers in the grid, only those that will prove most useful in your daily work. If, for example, you are trading bonds with coupons ranging between 7 per cent and 9 per cent and maturities ranging between three and 10 years, by memorizing that portion of the grid, which comprises just twelve numbers (as shown in Figure 16.3), it is possible to work out the approximate yield for a given price. You could

	7%	8%	9%
3 years	38	39	40
5 years	25	25	26
7 years	19	19	20
10 years	14	15	16

Figure 16.2   Modified duration grid for bonds of 3-10 years with coupons between 7 per cent and 9 per cent

then calculate the yield-to-maturity of an 8 per cent, 7-year bond trading at 97½ per cent as approximately 8.475 per cent (19bp x 2.5 = 47.5bp).

Our duration grid is for bonds trading at or close to par. The change in yield for a 1 per cent move in price on bonds trading at a large discount or premium e.g. 85 per cent or 125 per cent, will be different. By how much, will depend on the coupon and maturity. Those who regularly trade deeply discounted bonds, could create grids which reflect the price range encountered in their market. Grids can save time and make it possible to take advantage of market opportunities before they disappear.

Duration-weighted hedging

Modified duration enables you to compare the price sensitivity of different bonds. It can therefore be used for finding the weighting ratios when hedging one bond with another bond that has a different coupon and/or maturity.

A perfect hedge is a situation whereby any change in interest rates produces identical profit and loss amounts on the respective long and short positions. Hedging however can be a very risky business, especially when it involves being long and short of securities with different coupons and/or maturities and/or different types of securities.

Yield curve risk

If you own a 3-year bond and sell short a 5-year bond as a hedge, you must be confident that the yield curve between three and five years will remain the same. If, for example, a lot of new issues in the 5-year area are expected, you might conclude that the yield curve between three and five years will become more positive, as a result of yields in five years going up whilst yields in three years remain the same. On the other hand, if inflation appeared to be under control, the currency was strong, and yield levels in the 5-year area were relatively attractive, you might conclude that any new supply would be easily absorbed by investors. With the latter scenario, you may conclude that the spread between three and five years will remain the same.

If you sell short 10-year bonds because the curve is expected to become more positive, you must be confident that a more positive curve will occur as a result of yields for 10-year bonds going up while yields for 5-year bonds stay the same—not as a result of yields for 5-year bonds going down!

If you expect the curve between five and ten years to become more positive by way of yields for 5-year bonds going down, and yields for 10-year bonds going up, then you might decide to buy 5-year bonds and sell short 10-year bonds. If your prediction is correct, you will make money from both your long and your short.

Spread risk

The examples above relate to intra-market hedges, where you are long and short in the same type of bonds. However, it is common for traders to hedge eurobond positions with government securities. For example, a trader may sell short US Treasuries as a hedge against a long position in a US$ eurobond. These trades are common because there is no eurobond futures contract, and because eurobond markets are not as liquid as government bond markets, due to the individual issue size being smaller.

Such trades however, are risky. I recall some houses selling short considerable amounts of 10-year US government bonds as a hedge against their being long in large amounts of a new 10-year eurobond issue. However, they ended up losing a fortune on both sides because continued issuance of 10-year eurobonds depressed the price of their long eurobond position, whilst a rally in the US government market, pushed up the price of their short position.

When taking this route, you must factor in any fundamental, technical and/or psychological forces that could adversely affect the spread between government yields and euro yields. If not, you could lose far more money from a hedge than if you were simply to liquidate at a discount from the market price, and be done with it.

Example ➤

■ How to hedge trades using modified duration:
If you own one million of a 6 per cent 5-year eurobond at par and sell short (as a hedge) one million of a 6 per cent 3-year eurobond at 99 per cent, and yield levels increase by 50bp in both three and five years, you would still lose money.

A 50bp increase in yield on your 5-year long position would result in a decrease in price of 2.08 per cent (50 / 24 = 2.08) to 97.92 per cent, and you would sustain a loss of 20,800.

A 50bp increase in yield on your 3-year short position would result in a decrease in price of 1.32 per cent (50 / 38 = 1.32), to 97.68 per cent and you would make a profit of 13,200.

This would not be a perfect hedge. Because the difference in maturity has not been taken into account, the loss on your long position would be greater than the profit on your short position.

In order to ensure that the profit and loss on both your long and short positions are the same, in the event of an interest rate change, you must always weight the trade. This is particularly important when trading in securities that have different maturities, although significant differences in coupon can also result in an imperfect hedge and, consequently, different profit and loss amounts for an identical change in yield.

Because modified duration can be used to compare the price sensitivity of different bonds, it can also be used to calculate weighting ratios when hedging.

If, for example, you own a 6 per cent 3-year bond at 100 per cent—which you cannot or do not want to sell—and you feel that interest rates could rise, you could hedge your long position by selling short another 3-year bond. However, if for some reason you did not want to sell short in the 3-year area, perhaps because there was not another liquid 3-year bond available, or because you believe 3-year yield levels will bear up well in a declining market, you might want to hedge by selling a 5-year bond. Assuming that you do, and choose to short a 6 per cent 5-year bond that is trading at 99 per cent, how many 5-year bonds do you need to sell short to create a perfect hedge?

The most accurate way to find this out is to calculate the modified duration for each security, and then divide the results by each other. This will give the correct weighting ratio.

The modified duration of a 6 per cent 3-year bond trading at 100 per cent is 2.63 and the modified duration of a 6 per cent 5-year bond trading at 99 per cent is 4.20

$$2.63 / 4.20 = 0.63$$

This means that for every one million 3-year bonds that you own, it will be necessary to sell short 630,000 5-year bonds to create a perfect hedge.

It does not matter which number is divided by the other, as long as you understand volatility and the correlation between coupons, maturities and yields. For example, $4.20 / 2.63 = 1.6$. This means that for every 1.6 million 3-year bonds that you own, you need to sell one million 5-year bonds.

As it is always necessary to buy or sell less of a longer bond and more of a shorter bond, try to memorize less of a longer bond and more of a shorter bond. It may seem a bit like being back at school to do this, but where there are rules it is as well to remember them, and memorizing is a common and effective way. As a trader, I memorized the relevant numbers in the duration grid so as to calculate yields in my head, and I recited 'less of a longer' and 'more of a shorter' so many times that it became like a mantra.

While the modified duration of each bond in the above example was properly computed, our duration grid would have sufficed because both bonds were trading at or close to par, and in reality it is difficult to trade in an odd amount.

If you tried to buy or sell, say, 632 bonds or 1603 bonds, a trader will invariably adjust the price against you to reflect the difficulty he could encounter when trying to liquidate the odd two or three bonds. The market operates in round lots (multiples of 100). Small pieces are a nuisance. The grid is therefore good enough for calculating weighting ratios for small transactions.

Example ➤
It will be seen from the grid that a 6 per cent 3-year bond will move by 1 per cent in price if the yield changes by 38bp, and that a 6 per cent 5-year bond will move by 24bp. 38/24 = 1.58 which, rounded up, becomes 1.6. 24/38 = 0.631 which, rounded down, becomes 0.63.

If you sold short 630,000 5-year bonds as a hedge, against a long position of one million 6 per cent 3-year bonds, and interest rates went up by 50bp, your respective profit and loss on each position would be identical or as close to it.

A 50bp increase in yield on your 6 per cent 5-year short position would push the price down by 2.083 per cent (50/24 = 2.083), resulting in a profit of 13,125 (630,000 x 2.083 = 13,125).

A 50bp increase in yield on your 6 per cent 3-year long position would push the price down by 1.316 per cent (50/38 = 1.316), resulting in a loss of 13,160 (1,000,000 x 1.316).

By weighting the trade, you have a near-perfect hedge. By dealing in the odd amounts to make the hedge perfect, the premium charged by the trader for the extra two or three bonds is likely to cost more than the difference in your profit and loss. In this example, the loss due to rounding up and down is 35 dollars, pounds, Deutschemarks, or whatever the currency happens to be, which is tiny given the amounts involved. The following are some examples of weighting ratios.

Long position	Short hedge position	
(38) 1 million 6% 3-yr bonds	(24) 631,579 6% 5-yr bonds	(24/38)
(38) 1 million 7% 3-yr bonds	(19) 500,000 7% 7-yr bonds	(19/38)
(18) 1 million 6% 7-yr bonds	(24) 1,333,333 6% 5-yr bonds	(24/18)
(24) 1 million 6% 5-yr bonds	(14) 583,333 6% 10-yr bonds	(14/24)
(14) 1 million 6% 10-yr bonds	(18) 1,285,714 6% 7-yr bonds	(18/14)

Remember – 'Less of the longer' (LL) and 'more of the shorter' (MS)!

Chapter 17

GLOSSARY FOR CHAPTER 17

Bund
An abbreviation for *Bundesobligationen*, i.e. a debt obligation of the German Government.

DSL
Dutch State Loan, i.e. a debt obligation of the Dutch Government.

DTB
Deutsche Terminbörse, the Frankfurt exchange where financial futures are traded.

fungibility
Where contract specifications and trading and settlement procedures are identical, so that the same contract can be bought on one exchange and sold on another. In the context of bonds, it relates to whether subsequent tranches of an issue are identical and therefore interchangeable with the initial tranche.

futures
An abbreviation for futures contract. Futures contracts exist for commodities, currencies and indexes, as well as financial instruments.

LIFFE
London International Financial Futures & Options Exchange, the London exchange where financial futures are traded.

MATIF
Marché à Terme International de France, the Paris exchange where financial futures are traded.

notional bond
Theoretical bond.

overhanging
An abbreviation for *overhanging the Street*, i.e. when large amounts of securities are still in professional hands and yet to be distributed to investors.

tick
The minimum price change on a futures contract.

Chapter 17

Government futures: Hedging and basis trading

The yield of an international security is determined by yield levels in the underlying domestic market, with adjustments made for differences in structure, credit quality, liquidity, tax treatment of interest income, etc.[1] It is rare for an international security to trade at a lower yield than that available on the equivalent government security, although it does happen. If a borrower only comes to the market occasionally, their securities may have 'scarcity value', and trade very expensively because they perform well, relatively speaking, in both good and bad markets due to limited supply.

Yields of US$ eurobonds therefore, relate to yields available in US government securities with the same maturities. In the same way, yields of euro-Deutschemark and euroguilder bonds are influenced by yields in the German (Bund) and Dutch (DSL) government markets.

Consequently, and as there is not a eurobond futures contract, eurobond traders often use government futures as a substitute, particularly for hedging purposes.

Hedging a long euro position using government futures

This section introduces certain facts about futures markets, and in particular Bund futures. Please bear in mind however, that each futures contract has its own individual specifications. Be aware also, that it is not possible to buy a Bund contract on LIFFE (London International Financial Futures & Options Exchange) for example, and sell it on the DTB (German) or MATIF (French) exchanges. This may change, though, in the same way the specifications for the Bund contract could also change. Thus, before putting on any futures trade, make sure that you have up-to-date information on contract specifications, fungibility, trading limits, settlement procedures, etc.

---

[1] See 'Market anomalies: determinants of price' in Chapter 9.

The following example of how to hedge a long euro-Deutschemark position with German government bond futures is built around a hypothetical market situation, but one which could occur.[1]

You own 10 million of a recently issued 7 per cent, 7-year euro-Deutschemark bond at a price of 99 per cent, for a yield of 7.19 per cent. There are still a lot of bonds in professional hands which is discouraging buyers. You expect this bond to perform well once the surplus supply is placed with investors, and for this to take at least one month. While wanting to continue owning this bond, you do not want to be exposed to adverse market movements.

This example assumes that due consideration has been given to both spread risk and yield curve risk (see last chapter).

Firstly, you decide to hedge by selling short the most current Bund futures contract. This is possible, at a yield of 6¾ per cent, via LIFFE. The most current contract is the one that settles the soonest and which will most closely reflect movements in the Bund cash market. There are contracts for March, June, September and December. Each settles on the 10th day (or the next working day if the 10th is not a good business day) of the relevant month. The last trading day is usually the 7th.

The Bund contract is based on a notional 6 per cent bond with 8½ - 10 years remaining to maturity. A price factor is therefore used to convert bonds with coupons and maturities different from this so they can be delivered in settlement. The price factor is simply the price at which the actual bond to be delivered will yield 6 per cent. *Price Factor Tables*, available from exchanges for each contract they trade, contain price factors for all bonds acceptable for delivery.

To ensure that you are perfectly hedged you *must* weight your trade.

As you may remember, to do this you must find out the yield change for a 1 per cent move in price for both the eurobond you are long and the government bond you intend to sell. The coupon and maturity of the range of securities which are acceptable for delivery in settlement of a futures contract could be different from that of the notional bond. Using the average yield change for a 1 per cent move in price for all deliverable bonds is one option. Another is to use the cheapest deliverable bond, the one that creates the most profit or the least loss for the seller. This is the one most likely to be delivered on settlement date. Technical situations,

---

[1] *To be able to follow this example, you will need to have read Chapter 16.*

such as preferences among investors for certain coupons and/or maturities, can cause a lack of supply in a particular security. This can make one deliverable bond more expensive than another.

There is very little difference, however, in the duration of deliverable bonds with similar coupons and maturities. For instance, on any bond with a coupon between 6 per cent and 7 per cent, and a maturity between 8½ and 10 years, a 1 per cent move in price will change the yield by approximately 14bp. If however, the most actively-traded deliverable bonds were bonds with high coupons, perhaps because interest rates had risen, the duration could be a few basis points higher.

For this example we will assume the yield change for a 1 per cent price change is 14bp on your short position and 19 basis on your long position (as per the duration grid, assuming a coupon of 7 per cent in both cases).

The weighting ratio is therefore 0.737 (14 / 19 = 0.737).

This means that, for every one million 7-year euro-Deutschemark bonds you own, you need to sell the equivalent of 737,000 Bunds for the trade to be properly weighted. As you own DM10mm 7-year bonds you need to sell futures contracts to the value of DM7,370,000. The nominal amount of one Bund futures contract is DM250,000.

Although 7,370,000 divided by 250,000 equals 29.48, you can't sell 29.48 contracts! As 'round', as opposed to 'odd' lots are easier to trade, you decide to sell 30, rather than 29, contracts. You sell 30 contracts at 95.07 per cent, which is equal to a yield of 6¾ per cent on a notional 6 per cent bond with between 8½ and 10 years remaining to maturity. You are now long 10 million euro-Deutschemark bonds at a yield of 7.19 per cent and short the equivalent of 7,500,000 German government bonds at a yield of 6¾ per cent.

Margin funds

Margin funds are monies put up to show commitment to a trade, and as such are a sort of safety commitment to the clearing house or counterparty. Margin requirements are set by the various exchanges, and can and do change. The initial margin for Bund futures is currently DM6250 per contract.

If the market moves in your favour, excess margin will be released back to you. It is important to remember, however, that if your short futures position starts to run against you, more margin will have to be provided to the clearing house. Also, take into account that margin money is usually money borrowed and thus subject to interest, or at the very least, money upon which you could be earning interest. This example does not factor in interest costs or opportunity costs on margin funds.

You are now hedged, thus if interest rates do go up, the price of your long position will go down. Any loss, however, should be offset by a profit on your short position. Conversely, if interest rates fall, and the price of your long position goes up, any profit should cover the loss on your short futures position. Therefore, before selling your long position, unwind your hedge.

If interest rates go down (and prices up) and you can buy your futures contracts back at 95¼ per cent, at what price would you need to sell your euros in order to break even? Remember, you sold 30 of the March contract at 95.07 per cent. By buying back your futures at 95¼ per cent, you will incur a loss of 18 ticks, which on the Bund contract is the equivalent of 18bp as prices are quoted as a percentage of the underlying amount, to two decimal places. A *tick* is the minimum price movement in a futures contract, but it is not always equivalent to a basis point.[1] Each tick = DM25 (250,000 x .01 / 100 = 25). Your total loss, therefore, is 18 ticks x DM25 x 30 contracts = DM13,500.

13,500/10 million = DM1350 loss per one million euro-Deutschemark bonds.

To break even, and recoup the money lost on your futures trade, it will be necessary to sell your euros at no less than 99.135 per cent. You can sell out your long position in smaller pieces. If, for example, the opportunity arose to sell one million euros, you could buy back three contracts. If you could sell 1mm euros at 99.20 per cent and buy back three contracts at 95.35 per cent you would lose DM2100 on your futures (28 ticks x DM25 x 3 contracts) versus making a profit of DM2000 on your euros, resulting in a net loss of DM100.

If your prediction is correct, and interest rates rise and the price of your euro position goes down to 98½ per cent, at what price would you need to buy back the futures contracts to break even?

You would lose a total of DM50,000 on your 10 million euro position (a ½ per cent per million bonds). 50,000 divided by 30 (contracts) divided by DM25 (the value per tick) = 67 ticks. You would need to buy the futures back at 94.40 per cent (67 ticks lower than 95.07).

With the exception of *cash and carry* trades (*see* 'Basis trading', overleaf), it is easier and thus the norm, to close out a futures position prior to settlement date, rather than take/make delivery on the underlying security.

[1] *A tick in the futures market is not always a basis point. For instance, in the long gilt contract traded on LIFFE, a tick is equal to 1/32 per cent. For US Treasury bonds a tick is equal to 1/64 per cent. The underlying principal amount upon which a futures contract is based, and the tick value varies from contract to contract. Make sure that you know the precise specifications of a contract before you trade.*

However, the procedure for calculating the proceeds should you ever need to, is:

Futures settlement price × price factor × nominal amount plus accrued interest.

Basis trading

As traders who hedge with government bonds are in a position to identify what is known as *cash and carry* or *basis trading* opportunities, they often do such trades as an 'add-on' activity. There are two possible cash and carry trades to be done at any time:

a) Long bonds, short futures
b) Short bonds, long futures

The second is usually more costly because of borrowing costs and the availability of borrowable bonds. Consequently, the most popular basis trade is to short the futures and look for the cheapest bond to deliver against it. The following is an example using Bund futures:

Example ➤

a) You buy one million of a 10-year German government (Bund) 6½ per cent bond at 99½ per cent, to yield 6.57 per cent. On settlement date, the bond has six months' accrued interest on it.
b) You borrow money to finance this purchase at 5½ per cent.
c) You sell four Bund futures contracts at 97.00, to yield 6.42 per cent.

Assume this contract settles in 43 days and the price conversion factor to calculate settlement proceeds is 1.036800. Excluding margin costs, how much would you make or lose from doing this trade?

a)	b)	c)
Minus	**Plus**	**Plus or Minus**
cash price paid for bond	futures price × conversion factor	coupon income less finance costs
1,027,500	1,005,696	+33,514.00

a) The price at which you bought in the cash market, e.g. 99½ per cent plus 180 days' accrued interest at 6½ per cent = total proceeds paid out of DM1,027,500.

b) 1.036800 multiplied by the futures price of 97 per cent equals total proceeds received of DM1,005,696.00.

c) On settlement you will also receive 223 days' accrued interest at $6\frac{1}{2}$ per cent, amounting to DM40,263.89. After subtracting your financing costs of DM6750 ($5\frac{1}{2}$ per cent for 43 days on the total amount borrowed: 1,027,500 x .055 x 43 / 360). This leaves you with a net gain of DM33,514.00.

Minus 1,027,500 plus 1,005,696 plus 33,514.00 = **11,710 profit.**

Note: This example does not consider loss of opportunity on margin funds which are recalculated daily, based on the closing price of the futures contract. Remember, if your short futures position starts to run against you, it will be necessary to provide more collateral (cash) to the clearing house.

Note also, that taxation, commissions and liquidity are all extra considerations which can push/pull these type of trades either way throughout the life of a contract.

In strategies such as the one outlined above, basis traders often open one side, but not the other—taking a view on how the basis will change over the life of the trade. They calculate the implied repo rates for all deliverable bonds continually and, at delivery, choose the one with the lowest cash market value to the futures. The implied repo rate is the difference between the price of securities in the cash and futures market, expressed as an interest rate.

Chapter 18

GLOSSARY FOR CHAPTER 18

bankers' acceptance
Bills of exchange that are 'accepted' and therefore guaranteed by a bank or trust company. A type of guarantee of business done with manufacturers and exporters but not yet paid for, which they in turn pledge to a bank as collateral in return for a percentage of face value, to avoid cash-flow problems and enable them to continue doing business.

dead money
Money on which no interest is being earned.

FRAs
Forward Rate Agreements.

'off market' swap
A swap involving odd amounts. In the context of bonds 'off-market' can refer to a price that is wrong or to a switch transaction where the prices of the respective securities are marked up or down and do not therefore reflect the prices where business can legitimately be done. Note however that firms are legally required to trade at prices prevailing at the time of execution.

par bond
A bond trading at or close to 100 per cent of face value.

spot rates
Prices for spot rather than future settlement.

swap curve
A graphical illustration of swap rates for different periods.

swap rate
In the FX market, the swap rate is the difference between the spot and forward rates at which a currency is traded. In the context of an interest rate swap it is the fixed rate of interest a dealer will pay or receive in return for a floating rate of interest.

Treasury yield
The yield of a US government bond.

unwind

The process of reversing an existing position, either by liquidating or by entering into off-setting transactions.

zero curve

A graphical illustration of yields available on zero-coupon securities for different periods.

Chapter 18

Interest rate swaps

Market participants and their objectives

Many new issues that come to the market are interest rate and/or currency-swap driven. Interest rate swaps account for approximately 85 per cent of all swap activity. They enable market participants (borrowers, investors and the Street) to take advantage of the anomalies that arise due to their differing objectives, constraints, perceptions and expectations.

Borrowers use swaps to obtain their desired liability in terms of structure and currency, and/or to reduce the overall cost of raising money. Investors use them to obtain their desired asset in terms of creditworthiness, structure, currency, and/or to increase the rate of return. The Street intermediate between the two groups, as well as trade for their own account using their own capital.

The most active swap dealers include commercial banks and investment banks. Those involved play various roles. Some devote a lot of capital, and run substantial swap books as principal, often acting as the 'other side' of a trade. Others run smaller books and concentrate on arbitraging between markets.

Smaller houses, due to insufficient capital and/or credit standing, generally broker deals to facilitate business; rather than lose a mandate due to an uncompetitive swap rate, or not having a swap capability at all, it can make sense to find an acceptable swap counterparty for a client. You will often see a new deal, where one house does the swap because they had the best swap rate, while another lead manages the transaction because they had the best bond bid. A house with both syndicate and swap capabilities has the advantage, as both departments can work together to fine-tune the structure and/or pricing of a deal to meet a borrower's objective.

Institutions with the best credit rating and the biggest balance sheet, are the most sought after as swap counterparties, though they do sometimes price themselves out of the market. Like many markets, the swap markets are very competitive. If a borrower or investor can achieve a better swap rate from a bank with a slightly lower—but still acceptable—rating, then they may do so to save money.

Credit and interest rate risk

An interest rate swap involves an exchange of cashflows calculated on one particular interest basis, for those calculated on another basis. The most common is fixed rate flows for Libor flows and vice versa. Cashflows to be exchanged are based on an agreed underlying amount, usually par. Swaps on amounts other than par can be done, though are regarded as *off-market* swaps, which are discussed in more detail later in this chapter.

Interest rate swaps do not involve any exchange of principal. It is only the interest payments that are swapped. The risks however, are still considerable. The creditworthiness of a swap counterparty is of paramount importance. It is essential to be confident that the entity with whom you enter an agreement to swap cashflows on certain dates in the future, will actually still exist and be able to honour their side of the bargain for the life of the agreement.

As important of course, is profit, which comes from managing risk effectively. The commitment to receive or pay fixed-rate money, represents the greatest risk. Profits would be minuscule if, every time a dealer did a trade, he immediately hedged out all the risk (entered into a reciprocal agreement). Anyway, in reality, this is not always possible, which is one of the reasons why swap dealers take positions in the first place. An ability to anticipate changes in the shape of the yield curve, and spread relationships between fixed- and floating-rate funds, positioning themselves accordingly, is far more crucial. Indeed, this is where the big profits come from.

In contrast to the fixed rate commitment, the floating-rate commitment of a swap does not present any imminent risk, because Libor is never expressed as a specific rate. As long as the reset formula and the period for which it will apply (the reset interval) is agreed, any risk can be offset in the interbank or futures market nearer to the reset date.

How swaps are quoted and what the numbers mean

US$ swap rates can be quoted in relation to Treasuries or as an absolute rate. For example, the following quotes appeared on Reuters for two-year US$ swaps:

Term	Treasury yield	Spread	Annual - actual/360
2-yr	7.55-7.56	38-41	7.98-8.01

Term		Spread	Annual - actual/360
2-yr		40-37	8.01-7.97

The bid rates, 7.98 per cent and 7.97 per cent, respectively, are what each dealer is prepared to pay on a fixed-rate basis in return for receiving Libor. The offer rates, 8.01 per cent in both cases, are what each dealer will require in fixed-rate payments in return for paying Libor. Neither mentions Libor however, or the particular Libor period. In the context of swaps, any reference to Libor is usually to six-month Libor.

You will also see that, in the first example, the bid is followed by the offer while, in the second, the offer is quoted first. There is no convention in the way swap dealers present their rates. Just remember that the higher rate is the ask or offered rate, which is the fixed rate that must be paid to the swap dealer in return for receiving Libor. The lower rate is the fixed rate that the swap dealer will pay in return for receiving Libor.

In the second example, the two-year US Treasury yield is not included, but the spread in relation to US Treasuries is, though there is no mention of how interest is calculated or paid on US Treasuries which can be confusing.

US Treasuries pay interest semi-annually on an actual/actual basis. Thus, the annual rate of 7.98 per cent in the first example was arrived at by adding the Treasury yield of 7.55 per cent to the swap spread of 38bp, converting the result from semi-annual to annual, and then converting the yield to an actual/360 basis.

7.55 + .38 = 7.93 semi-annual, which equals 8.087 per cent annual.[1]
8.087/365 x 360 = 7.98 per cent on an actual/360 basis.

Always check the basis upon which interest is calculated, as any profit or yield pick-up could be more than eradicated if the day basis is different from what you thought.

How swaps are priced

Swaps are priced using a zero curve, derived from an underlying swap curve.

Calculation of a zero curve

Swap rates in one year are 9 per cent, and the two-year swap rate is 10.50 per cent. On an underlying amount of par, the fixed cashflows from the swap will be 10.5 in Year One and 110.5 in Year Two. To calculate the zero curve, first find the present value of the cashflow due in the first year. It is then possible to solve for the rate to be used to discount back the cashflow

[1] *See Chapter 11 for formula to convert yields from semi-annual to annual.*

due in the following year. Assuming annual compounding on a bond basis, the zero rate for Year One of a swap, is the same as the one-year swap rate, in this case 9 per cent. A zero rate is the rate of interest you will receive per year, multiplied by the underlying amount. It is therefore a simple annual interest rate, a sort of 'what you see is what you get' rate, so that 10 per cent on an underlying amount of 1000 will equal 100. Whether there are 365 or 366 days in a year is disregarded. This is the same method used to calculate interest on eurobonds, hence the reference to *bond basis*.

$$\frac{10.5}{(1+.09)^1} = 9.6330$$

Thus, the one-year zero rate is 9 per cent and the corresponding present value, 9.6330. But what is the two-year zero rate?

$$100 - 9.6330 = 90.367$$

$$\sqrt{\frac{110.5}{90.367}} - 1 = 10.5799$$

The two-year zero rate is therefore 10.5799 per cent, and the present value of the cashflow in Year Two is 9.9245.

Finding the zero curve for longer-dated swaps, involves a continuation of the above process. Thus, you are always solving for the rate for the next period that will produce a present value amount, which, when added to the present value amounts for the preceding periods, will equal par.

Although two years was used in the last example—to illustrate the concept as simply as possible—to price a short dated swap, a dealer would need to be conversant with yield levels for all similar and equivalent instruments. This would include FRAs, futures, Treasury bills, commercial paper, bankers' acceptances, cash deposits etc., yet this information would be of little use when dealing beyond two years. Since the money market is transparent, and a wide variety of instruments already exist to satisfy the needs and wants of both borrowers and investors, there is little to gain—and potentially a lot to lose—from trading short-dated swaps on an occasional basis, or in isolation from similar comparable instruments. Since the bulk of profits from money market trades comes from volume of transactions rather than a wide bid/offer spread, a swap dealer would need to trade all money market instruments full-time to make it worthwhile financially. His time is far better spent concentrating on the part of the curve where he can make the biggest difference and earn the most profit. The majority of swap activity therefore occurs between two and 10 years, although swaps can be done for as far out as 30 years.

Calculating a zero curve is not something one can do easily longhand. A financial calculator or spreadsheet is therefore helpful.

A dealer's zero curve is proprietary information, known only to the dealer, although it will be derived from spot rates and will perfectly equate to the swap rate.

A US$ swap rate for example, will reflect interest rates in government securities (including par bonds, Treasury strips and principal-only securities), futures and FRA markets for the same period. No one set of interest rates are formed in a vacuum, or used as a sole benchmark to dictate interest rates in another market. Everything is circular. All markets feed off, support, and reflect, each other. If interest rates in one product or currency do not equate to other equivalent products with similar characteristics and maturities, an arbitrage opportunity will exist. When this does in fact happen, the majority of anomalies are usually ironed out within minutes by professional arbitrageurs, thereby bringing the markets back into line.

Because a bond's price (the sum total of the present values of all cashflows) is calculated by discounting back each cashflow by 1 plus the yield, it implies the same reinvestment rate throughout. However, this is not actually the case. The zero curve for a two-year par bond with a 10 per cent coupon, will be the same as for a two-year 10 per cent swap rate. While the yield-to-maturity (YTM) calculation looks as if each cashflow is discounted back at the same rate, all that is actually happening is that the spot or zero curve has been rearranged to equate to a single, annually-compounded, interest rate.

Thus, while a resulting price will be the same, the present value amounts that make up that price will be different for each method. The yield curve for a par security will always equal the relevant spot rates. And the price of a coupon bond trading at par will be the same, whether the cashflows are discounted back using spot rates, or 1 + the yield.

The YTM concept is not the only method one can use to evaluate a par instrument, but as it is both simple to understand and to calculate, it has become universally accepted by the market.

Unwinding an off-market swap

A zero curve enables dealers to calculate accurate present value amounts for an entire swap curve. This enables a dealer to price off-market swaps just as easily as par swaps, and to calculate quickly the amounts required to unwind existing swaps.

For example, assume you are a swap dealer and that you entered into a swap with a client three years ago, agreeing to pay 13 per cent fixed for five years on an underlying amount of US$1,000,000. Your client would now like to unwind the swap by settling in cash, and would like to know how much money you would pay him to eliminate the agreement. Your two-year offered rate is 10½ per cent. The difference is therefore 2½ per cent for two years, and your zero curve is 9 per cent and 10.58 per cent for Years One and Two, respectively.

$$0.025 \times 0.09 \times 1,000,000 = US\$2250.00$$

$$0.025 \times .1058 \times 1,000,000 = US\$2645.00$$

US\$4895 would be the starting point. You may then decide to add or deduct an amount, depending on your view of the market, and interest in doing the trade.

If the underlying amount of the swap was US\$500,000, simply multiply by 500,000 rather than 1,000,000. However, the quoted swap rate will invariably be adjusted for an off-market swap. Whether one is dealing in a bond or a swap, an odd amount is harder to unwind. A premium or discount is usually added or subtracted from the quoted price or rate, to reflect the inconvenience and genuine difficulty one can encounter when trying to liquidate an odd amount.

Although a swap dealer's zero curve is proprietary information known only to him, one can roughly gauge what a payment or swap rate should be from the relevant spot rates, and where interest rates are on equivalent products. Any difference will be a function of supply and demand, and a dealer's interest in doing a particular trade. Major houses usually have thousands of swaps on their book at any one time, and are constantly unwinding and rearranging the flows to reflect their market view. Another factor influencing swap rates is capital adequacy guidelines, which require a percentage of the full value of a swap to be kept in reserve, as a safeguard against any defaults. The 'opportunity cost' of 'dead' money has therefore to be built into a dealer's swap rate.

Asset swaps

An asset swap involves buying an asset and swapping the cashflows that arise from it. The most common trade is to purchase a fixed-rate bond and enter into a swap agreement to change the bond's structure from fixed to floating rate. Asset swaps are usually presented as a package at a specific yield at a price of par.

A client will not know whether they are paying 95 per cent for a bond and five points to the swap dealer, or 94½ per cent to the bond dealer, four points to the swap dealer, and 1½ points to an asset swap trading desk within the same firm. All the client will know is that if they pay par they can achieve a yield of x, which will involve their buying a particular asset and passing the cashflows from that asset to the swap dealer. In return, the swap dealer will pay the client interest on another basis, the most common exchange being fixed-rate flows for Libor flows, or vice versa.

Asset swaps can be done for partial periods. A client could buy a five year bond, but only do a swap for the first two years. In such cases though, they would assume yield-curve risk for the remaining period, following expiration of the swap agreement.[1]

Example ➤
New issue swap.
Assume you are representing the borrowing entity. You want to borrow $100mm on a floating-rate basis for three years, at an all-in cost of Libor plus 5bp (assume 'all-in' to mean inclusive of interest charges and issuing commissions/fees). If you issue a straightforward FRN, your all-in costs will be Libor plus ¼ per cent, which is very expensive, given your credit standing. This is not a viable option therefore because:

a) you are not prepared to pay this much, and,
b) to do so could set a precedent and increase your borrowing costs the next time you come to the market.

FRN investors either do not know your company well or perhaps they cannot, for various reasons, buy into your industry. Or perhaps the market simply cannot cope with another new issue. Whatever the reasons, the FRN market is effectively closed to you for the moment. The fixed-rate market however is more promising in that you could issue a three-year fixed rate bond with a 6¼ per cent coupon, at par, with ³⁄₁₆ per cent fees and ⅛ per cent issuing expenses, to give you an all in cost, when rounded up, of 6.37 per cent:

To work out an all-in cost as a rate of interest, involves an iterative process, i.e. finding the rate which, when all the cashflows in Years One, Two and Three, are discounted back, will produce a present value amount of, in this case, $99,687,500.

+ $ 99,687,500   (After deducting .3125 for fees and issuing expenses)
- $ 6,250,000   Interest payment at the end of Year One
- $ 6,250,000   Interest payment at the end of Year Two
- $106,250,000   Interest payment, plus principal, at the end of Year Three

IRR = 6.3677 per cent annual

[1] *See subsections on 'Yield curve risk' and 'Spread risk' in Chapter 16.*

You can, however, approximate an IRR when dealing with a par, or close to par amount, using our duration grid. As you will see from the grid (Figure 16.1 in Chapter 16), a one-point move in price on a par bond with either a 6 per cent or 7 per cent coupon, will change the yield by 38bp. A price move of ⁵⁄₁₆ per cent (.3125) will therefore change the yield by 11.875bp which, when added to the coupon of 6¼, equals a YTM of 6.3687 per cent. Grids can save a lot of time!

If you receive 6.30 per cent fixed rate in return for paying the swap house six-month Libor, but the all-in cost of your fixed-rate deal is 6.37 per cent, you would lose seven basis points on that side, which would push your floating-rate cost of funds up to Libor plus seven basis points. On a 100mm dollar deal, two basis points would cost you an extra US$20,000 per year in interest charges. Any difference in the basis upon which the interest flows of a swap are calculated, could also make a significant difference. Always check that they are on the same basis and if not, convert one side so that you have an accurate picture. While Libor flows are almost always calculated actual/360, there is no convention with regard to fixed rate flows. These could be actual/360 or 30/360.

New issue swap - a case study

Rabobank Nederland NV, the AAA/Aaa-rated Dutch bank, issued four-year fixed-rate US dollar debt which was reported in the press to have been swapped into floating-rate US dollars, at six-month Libor minus 25bp (0.25 per cent).

As a result of the bond issue and the interest rate swap, Rabobank created floating-rate debt at a cheaper price than would have been possible by issuing floating-rate debt, either through an FRN or through the syndicated loan market. If the cost of issuing floating-rate funds through an FRN is Libor minus 5bp, then the saving to Rabobank of issuing fixed-rate debt and swapping to floating is 20bp:

	All in cost to Rabobank
Fixed-rate debt (swapped to floating)	6-month USD Libor - 0.25%
Floating-rate note (all-in cost)	6-month USD Libor - 0.05%
Net saving to Rabobank	0.20%

When this arbitrage opportunity exists, it encourages many well-rated borrowers to issue fixed-rate debt and swap it to create cheaper floating-rate funds than would otherwise be possible. Rabobank's post swap cost of floating-rate funds is determined by the difference between its all-in cost of fixed-rate debt, and the swap rate available in the market:

	% s.a. 30/360
4-yr USD IRS (vs. 6-month USD Libor)	Plus 7.66
All-in cost (4-year fixed-rate issue)	Minus 7.41

Post-swap cost	6-mth USD Libor	Less 0.25%

Both of these rates can be expressed as spreads over a benchmark. If you subtract the four-year Treasury yield (T) from both the swap rate (7.66 s.a.) and the all-in cost of Rabobank's fixed-rate debt (7.41 s.a.). If $T = 7.28$ then the rates can be expressed as follows:

	% semi-annual actual/actual
4-yr USD IRS (vs. 6-month USD Libor)	T +38
All-in cost (4-year fixed-rate issue)	T +13

Post-swap cost	6-mth USD Libor less 0.25%

Chapter 19

OPTION TERMS

American-style
An option which may be exercised on any day up to maturity.

at-the-money
Exercise price equals the price of asset in the cash market.

call option
The holder of a call option has the right to buy a specific amount of a specific security at a fixed price.

European-style
An option which may only be exercised at maturity.

exercise date
The date on which an option can be exercised. This differs depending on whether the option is *American- or European-style* (see below).

in-the-money
The option has exercise value i.e. the exercise or strike price is below (in the case of a call option), or above (in the case of a put option), the price of the underlying asset in the market.

intrinsic value
The value of an option due to it being in the money.

maturity
Final day on which an option may be exercised.

out-of-the-money
Exercise price lies above (in the case of a call), or below (in the case of a put), the prevailing price of the underlying asset.

premium
Price/cost of an option.

put option
The holder of a put option has the right to sell a specific amount of a specific security at a fixed price.

strike
Price at which the option may be exercised and the underlying security bought or sold (also known as *exercise price*).

time value
The value of the option based on the time remaining to maturity/expiration.

Chapter 19

Introduction to options

Options can in fact aid, rather than hinder, profitability, but they have come to be seen as daunting instruments because of the increasing number of stories about option-related losses. The downfall of an entire bank—Barings—is enough to scare anyone away. This chapter will introduce you to the principles of both stock and bond options, and the inherent risks.

An option is a derivative instrument which could not exist without the underlying instrument, but which has different characteristics from that of the underlying product on which it is based. A future is a derivative instrument, though as you would expect, there are differences between futures and options. The key to using options successfully, is to understand their characteristics and how they differ from those of the underlying product. Familiarize yourself with the option terms shown on the two previous pages before reading on.

Key factors influencing an option's price

The main determinants of the price of an option according to the 'Black & Scholes' model, the industry standard, are:

1) Volatility
2) Time
3) Short-term interest rates
4) Strike price
5) Current price

While the last two are self-explanatory, the first three require some clarification.

Volatility

Consider three shares, A, B and C, all trading at 120 each. If you could buy a call option (i.e. the right to buy) at a strike price of 140 on all three shares, which one would you buy, assuming the premium (e.g. cost) was the same for all three?

You would choose the share that has historically displayed the greatest swings in price. The key to option markets is volatility. It does not matter if the price goes back to its original value by the expiration date, as long as it moves up and down a lot in-between. The greater the swings, the more chance that the option could move 'in-the-money' at some point.

Volatility measures the vulnerability of the underlying market to significant price moves up or down. The greater the volatility, the more uncertainty there is about the direction and speed of price movements in the underlying product. For example, fears about major events (strikes, wars, elections etc.) are usually more immediately noticeable in the option markets through a rise in volatility.

Time

If you were told that you could buy a car for $10, with the only provision being that you had to find one painted in 'Canary Yellow', you would no doubt be thrilled. However, if you were told to find one within 30 seconds, you would be less happy than if you had 30 days. While this may seem unrelated to the world of finance, it illustrates that the time remaining to expiration of an option has value. However, for European-style options on debt instruments (bonds), this is not always the case, as much depends on short-term interest rates.

Short-term interest rates

Consider a steepening yield curve environment, where the differential between short- and long-term rates is widening, with longer-term rates increasing at a faster pace than short-term rates.

With a European-style call option on a bond, the longer the maturity of the option, the greater the risk that interest rates will be higher come the exercise date. This would consequently lower the price of the bond at that time.

It would not help to look at current three-year interest rates, to evaluate a one-year European option to convert into a three-year bond. Instead, consider three-year rates in one year's time. American options are different as they can be exercised at any time. This sometimes makes them more valuable, though they can also be harder to value, given the uncertainty about the exercise date.

In the event of wanting to buy some shares in stock X, rather than investing immediately, it may be more profitable to buy an American call option on the shares, exercise it on the last possible date, and invest the cash in the meantime. In this way, some interest income may be earned.

The Black & Scholes Model can be, and is, used to value bond options, but adjustments are usually made to reflect the fact that, unlike shares, the majority of bonds pay interest and mature at some point, usually at par. As the price of a bond must converge to par by its maturity date, and may pay interest in-between, its price volatility will be different from that of a share.

For those interested in understanding more about futures and options, I would recommend *Introduction To Futures And Options Markets* by John Hull, and also *An Introduction to Commodity Futures & Options* by Nick Battley. Full details can be found in the Bibliography.

Buying options - the downside

When going long of options, you are buying the right to: buy (in the case of a call), or sell (in the case of a put), the underlying product, such as a currency, bond or share, at a pre-determined price for a certain pre-determined time. The premium paid is, in many ways, a form of insurance. If the underlying market moves in your favour through the strike price, it is possible to exercise your option, liquidate the resulting position in the cash market, and book a profit. If it does not, then your option will expire unexercised and all that is lost is the premium. When buying options therefore, your downside is limited to the premium paid.

Selling options - the downside

When selling an option you receive premium income. If the option is *covered*, your downside is limited, but could still be a lot more than the premium received. If the option is *naked*, your downside is unlimited!

When the party to whom you sell a call option decides to exercise it, you are obliged to sell the underlying product to them at the strike price. In the same way, when the party to whom you sell a put option decides to exercise it, you are obliged to buy the underlying product at the strike price. The loss would therefore be the difference between the market price and the strike price, less premium income received.

There is a lot more risk involved in selling (writing) options than buying options. While you may receive premium income, the downside could be far, far greater than any premium received. This is particularly true if the market moves substantially against you, which can easily happen. Option prices can move dramatically and quickly especially during periods of extreme volatility.

Covered calls

The least risky way to sell options is to write covered call options, which can be an attractive strategy in quiet markets.

By selling a call option on an underlying amount of bonds which you already own, you have written a covered call and are, in effect, hedged. Any loss will be limited to the market price at which you could have otherwise sold the bonds, less the premium income received. It is important however, to factor in any loss of opportunity on the money that is tied up. If, for example, you could have made more by simply selling the bonds and investing the proceeds elsewhere, rather than holding them and writing a call, you will not have achieved maximum profitability.

The premium income from a covered call should adequately compensate for being restricted from doing anything with the bonds for the life of the option. If the option expires unexercised, you will still own the bonds, but the cost price will, in effect, be reduced by the amount of premium received. If you essentially like the market and are happy to continue owning the bonds, but feel that interest rates could go up, writing a call option could make sense. The premium received would provide a cushion for a certain increase in yield.

Naked calls and puts

Writing naked options is extremely risky. To write a call option on an unowned asset, is to write a naked option. If exercised, you will have to fulfill your obligation and sell the underlying asset at the strike price. In the same way, if you write a put option and are exercised, you are obliged to purchase the underlying asset at the strike price. In both cases, the strike price may bear no relation to the prevailing market price for the underlying asset.

When the US stock market collapsed in 1987, those who had written put options on stocks or stock indexes lost vast amounts of money, as they were obliged to purchase securities at the strike prices. These were substantially higher than prevailing market prices.

Embedded options

Many bonds have been created over the years which, on close examination, contain options. Whenever you see a bond that looks unusual, go to your analyst. If there is an option included, it may be wrongly valued and provide an opportunity to make a profit. Some examples include:

■ Callable bonds:
These are bonds that give the issuer the right to call/redeem the bond at a date prior to maturity. An investor in a callable bond has effectively therefore bought a bond and also written a call, which should be compensated for in some way, such as by an increase in the bond's coupon.

Owning a bond that matures in five years, but which is callable in three years, is equivalent to owning a non-callable five-year bond and selling a two-year call option.

■ Puttable bonds
Puttable bonds give the investor the right to put the bond back to the issuer before the stated maturity date. Here the investor has bought a bond with a put option attached, in which case the coupon payable on the bond may be lower.

■ Convertible bonds
These are bonds that contain an option to convert the bond into equity. This is the equivalent of buying a low-coupon bond, plus an equity call option.

If a bond contains an embedded option in its structure, it is prudent to check the value of the option component. If it turns out to be inadequately valued in your favour, it may be possible to hedge out the embedded risk via other options and make some money in the process. If it is inadequately valued against you, then it may be prudent not to buy it, or if you already own it, to sell it.

Applications

Options offer the flexibility to undertake many types of transactions. Their main uses can be distilled down to variations upon the following three applications:

1) To hedge (reduce) risk;
2) To take advantage of market anomalies;
3) For speculation purposes.

Before dealing in options, do understand precisely your reasons for choosing options and what the upside and downside could be if all your predictions turn out to be completely wrong.

Key considerations

Before putting on an option position, it is essential to have a clear view on the underlying market. Then work out whether you want to buy or sell, and whether to buy or sell puts or calls. Then decide on your preferred maturity and strike price, both of which will affect the price of the option.

If an option's strike price differs considerably from the current market price, it will affect the premium. What is more important, however, as you may remember, is the likelihood of the price of the underlying product going through the strike price during the option's life. This makes the time-horizon very important too. The longer the maturity, the more the option will cost, although the relationship between time and price is not linear. For example, a one-year option is not twice as expensive as a six-month option.

Lastly, decide whether the premium paid or received adequately compensates for the risks involved. How much could you lose if your predictions are completely wrong? It is important to compare the upside versus the downside before putting on the position.

Be clear about market direction within a pre-determined time-frame. For example, if you buy a European-style two-month call option on a bond which is 2 per cent out of the money for a premium of 1 per cent of face value, you are in effect saying that, on the maturity date, you expect the market in the bond to have increased by at least 3 per cent. If the market does indeed improve by 3 per cent, but only after the option expires, you will lose the premium.

Summary

One of the key advantages of using an instrument such as an option is that, at its simplest, buying a call option makes it possible to take a one-way view on the underlying market in significant size, but without assuming enormous risk. The most you can lose is the premium paid. However, when it comes to writing options, exercise extreme caution and do not get carried away by the attraction of receiving premium income up-front.

Some points to remember when using options:

1) Be clear about your reasons for choosing options.
2) Be clear about the specifications of the option contract(s) chosen. For example, options on US Treasury note and bond futures, are based on an underlying amount of US$100,000, and the minimum price movement is $1/64$ per cent, i.e. $15.625 for a one-tick move. Options on three-month eurodollar futures are for an underlying amount of US$1,000,000 and the minimum price movement is $1/100$ per cent, i.e. $25 for a one-tick move $(1,000,000 \times 0.01 / 100 \times 90 / 360)$.
3) Do not pay more than necessary. You may be better off buying a shorter option with a lower premium, and then buying another one later.
4) Although buying options allows you to know the maximum downside in advance, buying an out-of-the-money option that decays to zero, will reduce your performance.
5) Do not be afraid to change your mind. Even if an option position is taken 'passively' many options are very liquid, and may still have value should it be desirable to unwind an option position.

6)   Simplicity is strength. Complicated strategies are for option specialists.
7)   The options market is a market. Whatever the theory, the ultimate price in any market is that which equates supply and demand.

Option theory is complicated. The purpose of this chapter has been to foster an intuitive, rather than an absolute, understanding of what determines an option's price, and provide an overview of the risks and rewards. While options can be used effectively to aid profitability, it is important to remember that they are complex instruments and, as such, can display what can appear to be irrational price behaviour. In particular, the volatility dimension of options can be underestimated, particularly by occasional users. For example, volatility hedging—which is a key component of risk management and comparable to duration-hedging in the bond markets—can be a complicated and potentially imperfect exercise, even for experts.

Chapter 20

GLOSSARY FOR CHAPTER 20

floaters
Colloquial term for FRNs.

long-dated FRN
FRNs with longer maturities relative to what is regarded by the market as normal. This can change.

short-dated FRNs
FRNs with maturities of just a few years.

Chapter 20

Euro floating-rate notes (FRNs)

Libor as a benchmark

The yield of a euro FRN is described in terms of its spread in relation to a chosen benchmark, usually Libor. In the US, the benchmark is usually US Treasury bills. Depending on the credit quality of the issuer, the spread on a euro FRN could be over, or under, Libor or Libid (London interbank bid rate) or Limean, which is the average of the two.

While the spread between Libid and Libor has been ⅛ per cent for many years (the Debt Crisis in 1982 excluded), this could change. It is important therefore to consider the way the yield in relation to Libor is described in the prospectus for a security, particularly when buying long-dated FRNs, such as perpetuals. For example, an FRN that resets at Libid plus ⅛ per cent may not always translate into Libor. If the spread between Libid and Libor widens to a ¼ per cent, the issue will effectively be set at Limean.

Method of evaluation

FRNs are commonly evaluated via what is known as the 'discount margin' method. This involves discounting all the cashflows back to their present value, to find the correct price for a given estimated yield. The process is similar to the calculation for fixed-rate securities, except with FRNs you do not know what the exact coupon payments will be. You must therefore make certain assumptions about where Libor will be over the life of the floater. Although you can find out the markets' expectations from the swaps and futures markets, your own may differ and so, therefore, will your assumptions. Also, what makes this calculation more fiddly rather than complex, is that interest on FRNs is calculated actual/360 (except eurosterling FRNs which are calculated actual/365), and there is more than one interest payment per year. Semi-annual and quarterly FRNs are the most common, although there are some that reset monthly (*see* Chapter 21).

Because the calculation for finding the price given the discount margin is rather cumbersome and can be a little confusing, I have decided to present you with two versions. The first version is a personal preference that I used when trading FRNs. The second is for those who find lengthy formulas easy to follow.

To find the price of an FRN a lot of information is required. This is listed below together with, in brackets, sample details which will be used for both examples.

- Current coupon (5 per cent)
- Number of days in current coupon period (182)
- Days remaining from settlement date to next coupon payment date (129)
- Cost of finance from settlement date to next coupon payment date (6.20 per cent)
- Spread in relation to Libor (plus ⅛ per cent)
- Estimated base Libor for the life (6 per cent)
- Number of compounding periods from next coupon date to maturity (5)
- Coupon reset frequency (every six months)
- Coupon payment frequency (every six months)

Using the above details, we are now going to solve for the correct price, for an estimated discount margin of 10bp above six-month Libor.

Discount margin calculation - Version One

This version is the simpler of the two, primarily because it does not start with a complicated formula. Instead, I have used smaller formulae for each stage, and have broken the calculation down into six steps.

■ Step One: Calculating future coupon payments

On a fixed-rate bond, coupon cashflows are known whereas, with an FRN, they are not—as it is not possible to know exactly where Libor will be over the life of a note. This is particularly true for long-dated FRNs. An assumed base Libor is therefore used.

$$(BL + RS) \times \frac{DP}{360} \times 100$$

where,

BL	assumed base Libor rate for the life (6 per cent)
RS	reset spread (plus ⅛ per cent)
DP	days in each whole compounding period (182.625*)

*182.625 days takes leap years into account

$$(0.06 + 0.00125) \times \frac{182.625}{360} \times 100 = 3.10716$$

Each coupon cashflow, is therefore made up of an assumed base Libor of 6 per cent plus the spread of ⅛ per cent, multiplied by 182.625/360 because coupons are paid semi-annually. A different Libor assumption for each period can be used if preferred.

■ Step Two: Finding the rate at which to discount cashflows back to their present value, as of the next coupon date.

With a fixed-rate bond, the price is found by discounting the cashflows back by 1 + the yield. It is the same with an FRN, except that the yield is made up of Libor plus the discount margin.

$$1 + (BL{+}DM) \times \frac{DP}{360}$$

where,

BL assumed base Libor rate (6 per cent)
DM estimated discount margin (10 basis points)
DP days in each whole compounding period

$$1 + \frac{(0.06 + 0.0010 \times 182.625^{*})}{360} = 1.0309448$$

*Use the exact number of days if preferred.

■ Step Three: Discounting cashflows back to present value, as of the next coupon payment date.

$$P = \frac{3.10716}{(1.0309448)^{1}} \; \frac{3.10716}{(1.0309448)^{2}} \; \frac{3.10716}{(1.0309448)^{3}} \; \frac{3.10716}{(1.0309448)^{4}} \; \frac{103.10716}{(1.0309448)^{5}}$$

3.0138956 + 2.9234306 + 2.8356810 + 2.7505653 + 88.534342

The sum total of these PV amounts is 100.05791. This is the present value of all future cashflows as of the next coupon date.

■ Step Four: Calculating and adding accrued interest

To 100.05791, add the coupon payment to be received in 129 days' time. The current coupon is 5 per cent and there are 182 days in the current coupon period, so the next coupon payment will be 2.52778, calculated as follows:

$$0.05 \times \frac{182}{360} \times 100 = 2.52778$$

$$100.05791 + 2.52778 = 102.58569$$

■ Step Five: Finding the rate at which to discount the sum total of all cash-flows back to present value

102.58569 must now be discounted back to present value by 1 + the rate that represents the cost of financing for the partial 129 days remaining in the current coupon period. The cost of financing is 6.20 per cent and thus the rate is 1.0222167, calculated as follows:

$$1 + (0.0620 \times \frac{129}{360}) = 1.0222167$$

■ Step Six: Discounting the sum total of all cashflows back to present value and deducting accrued interest

To discount back to present value, simply divide the sum total of all the cashflows by 1.0222167:

$$\frac{102.58569}{1.0222167} = 100.35611$$

100.35611 is the gross price and includes accrued interest, which needs to be deducted. There are 53 days' accrued interest at 5 per cent, so deduct 0.73611, calculated as follows:

$$(0.05) \times \frac{53}{360} \times 100 = 0.73611$$

$$100.35611 - 0.73611 = 99.62$$

Thus, the correct price for this FRN for an estimated discount margin of 10bp over six-month Libor, is 99.62 per cent.

Discount margin calculation - Version Two

The following formula for finding the price for a given estimated discount margin, follows ISMA's method detailed in their book *Formulae for Yield and Other Calculations* (see Bibliography for details).

$$\sum_{k=1}^{n} \frac{c_{n} * 365.25/360}{\frac{(1+(1+y)^{n}-1)^{k-1}}{2n} + tsc/360} + \frac{F}{\frac{(1+(1+y)^{n}-1)^{N-1}}{2n} + tsc/360}$$

where,

P	gross (dirty) price
N	number of coupons
n	number of coupons per annum
y	Libor plus discount margin (in decimal)
tsc	days remaining from settlement date to next coupon payment date
F	redemption price (in decimal)

As in the previous example, this approach also involves discounting all cashflows back to their present value as of the next coupon date, then discounting the sum total of these amounts back to present value, then deducting the accrued interest.

1) $.05 \times 182/360 = .02528$

This is the coupon payment for the current period which is due in 129 days' time.

2) $\dfrac{.06125 \times 365.25/360 \times 1/2}{1+(((1+0.061/2)^{2}-1)/2)} = \dfrac{.03107}{1.030965} = .03014$

Above the line, we have the expected Libor for the period of 6 per cent plus the spread of ⅛ per cent over Libor, making a total of 6⅛ per cent. We have multiplied by 365.25 to take leap years into account, divided by 360 to find the exact coupon due per annum, and multiplied by 1 over 2 to find the semi-annual coupon payment.

Below the line, we have the expected Libor for the period of 6 per cent plus the estimated discount margin of 10bp making a total of 6.10 per cent. To find the rate to be used to discount each cashflow back to its present value as of the next coupon date, we take 1 + the annual rate of 6.10 divided by 2 and then square it (remember that this is the formula used for finding the annual equivalent of a semi-annual yield). We then have to adjust for the fact that we are dealing with a semi-annual period, which is why we subtract 1, divide by 2 and add 1 to arrive at 1.030965. 1.030965 is therefore the discount rate to be used to bring all the coupon payments, and principal, back to their value as of the next coupon date.

3) $\dfrac{.06125 \times 365.25/360 \times 1/2}{(1+(((1+0.061/2)^2-1)/2))^2} = \dfrac{.03107}{1.030965^2} = .02923$

This is simply a repeat of (2) except that as we are dealing with the second complete compounding period, we raise the discount rate to the power of 2.

4) $\dfrac{.06125 \times 365.25/360 \times 1/2}{(1+(((1+0.061/2)^2-1)/2))^3} = \dfrac{.03107}{1.030965^3} = .02835$

Do the same as before, but discount back to the power of 3 as we are dealing with the third complete compounding period.

5) $\dfrac{.06125 \times 365.25/360 \times 1/2}{(1+(((1+0.061/2)^2-1)/2))^4} = \dfrac{.03107}{1.030965^4} = .02750$

The same again, but we discount back to the power of 4.

6)[1] $\dfrac{1+.06125 \times 365.25/360 \times 1/2}{(1+(((1+0.061/2)^2-1)/2))^5} = \dfrac{1.03107}{1.030965^5} = .88526$

$$\overline{1.02576}$$

7) 1.02576 is the sum total of all the cashflows *as of the next coupon date*. We must now discount this amount back to present value by the remaining 129 days in the current coupon period. The cost of of finance for 129 days is 6.20 per cent and thus the rate used to discount back to today's value is 1 + 6.20 raised to the power of 129 over 360, i.e. 1.0221212.

$$\dfrac{1.02576}{(1+((1+0.062/2)^2)^{129/360}} = \dfrac{1.02576}{1.0221212} = 1.00356$$

8) 1.00356 is the gross price and thus accrued interest needs to be deducted.

a) Gross price   =   1.00356

b) Less accrued interest: =   .00736 (0.05 × 53/360)

a − *b*   =   .99620

                    =   99.62%

---

[1] *As redemption also occurs when this coupon is paid, the principal must be included before discounting back to the power of five.*

Evidently, calculating the discount margin on an FRN is a lengthy process, and certainly, a personal computer will do the calculation faster. Nonetheless, it is useful to understand the steps involved.

Approximating the discount margin, given the price

The following is a quick way to approximate the discount margin on an FRN given the price.

Example ➤
A two-year FRN that resets and pays interest semi-annually at ⅛ per cent over Libor, which is trading at 99.80 per cent flat of accrued interest, will have a discount margin of approximately Libor plus 24bp, assuming a base Libor for the life of 6 per cent. This is calculated as follows:
12.5bp (the spread over Libor) plus 10bp (the discount from par divided by the remaining life, which assumes that the price will converge to par through equal adjustments at each reset date), plus additional interest of 1.2bp (because interest is received on par not cost price). 12.5 + 10.0 + 1.2 = 23.7bp.
Using either of the previous formulas, it will be found that for an estimated discount margin of Libor + 24bp the price is, in fact, 99.78 per cent:

$$P = \frac{3.10716}{(1.031655)^1} \quad \frac{3.10716}{(1.031655)^2} \quad \frac{3.10716}{(1.031655)^3} \quad \frac{103.10716}{(1.031655)^4}$$

$$3.0118208 + 2.9194070 + 2.8298288 + 91.022943 \quad = \quad 99.78\%$$

Example ➤
For this example, we will use the same details as in earlier examples, i.e. an FRN that resets and pays interest semi-annually at ⅛ per cent over Libor, with 2.86 years remaining to maturity.[1]

1) Calculate the negative or positive carry for the days remaining from settlement date to next coupon payment date. The price plus accrued interest as at settlement date was 100.36 per cent, i.e. 99.62, plus .74 accrued interest (0.05 x 53/360) = 100.36. The difference between the

---

[1] You may recall this was a three-year FRN as of 53 days ago and thus there are 311.625 days (182.625 days and 129 days) left in the current year. 311.625/360 = .86

current coupon (5 per cent) and the cost of finance (6.2 per cent) is 1.2 per cent.

100.36 x 0.012 x 129 / 360 = 0.43 negative carry.

2) Add or subtract positive or negative carry respectively. As, in this case, there is negative carry of .43, this amount should be added to the price. 99.62 plus .43 = 100.05. This is known as the *neutral price*.

3) Amortize any discount or premium from par over the remaining life, and add or subtract, respectively, from the stated spread in relation to Libor. As the bond is trading at a premium over the redemption price of 0.05, there is a loss of 1.7bp per year (0.05 / 2.86 = 1.7). The spread of ⅛ per cent over Libor should be reduced by this amount. 12.5 less 1.7 = 10.8bp.

4) Adjust for the fact that interest is only paid on par, not the cost price, which in this case is 100.05 per cent. By paying more than par, therefore, you will earn less than the stated interest whereas by paying less than par, you will earn more. Given an assumed base Libor of 6 per cent plus the spread of ⅛ per cent, there is a loss of 6⅛ per cent in interest on 0.05 in price. As the premium over par in this example is tiny, the loss in interest is only about a third of a basis point (0.06125 x 0.05 = .003). 12.5 less 1.7 less 0.3 = 10.5bp, approximately.

Although this is a rough method, it does enable you to calculate the approximate discount margin quickly.

Chapter 21

GLOSSARY FOR CHAPTER 21

CRD
Council of Reporting Dealers (an arm of ISMA)

Emu
European Monetary Union

ERM
Exchange rate mechanism, a system via which exchange rates between two or more currencies is controlled by the respective central banks.

Ecu
European currency unit. A unit of exchange based on a basket of European currencies which is set to become the common currency for Europe.

LDC
Less-developed countries, which now tend to be referred to as 'emerging' economies or markets, which is less derogatory.

Savings & Loans
The US equivalent of UK building societies.

Chapter 21

Avoiding disasters

T he following is my interpretation of the events which caused two significant eurobond market crises: the collapse of the floating-rate note market in 1986-87 and the Ecu bond market in 1992. Relative newcomers to the business should read this catalogue of events carefully, as I believe similar things could happen in other markets in the future. This chapter is intended to help you identify the alarm bells of an impending crisis.

The underlying emotions which caused both crises, followed the typical order: greed, fear and then self-preservation. Intellectually-advanced we may be, but emotionally-developed we are not. Our most primitive instincts still dominate, especially where money is involved.

Very little was learned from the FRN market crash. Many of the mistakes made in the run-up to the Ecu bond market collapse in 1992 were also made in the FRN market six years before. Undertaking post-mortems is both time-consuming and risky. The Street has little time, and whilst objective reflection can prove a tremendous learning experience, it can also expose extreme incompetence, often at a very senior level!

The FRN market crash 1986-87

In summary, I believe the FRN market collapsed because too many houses viewed it as a quick and profitable way to raise profiles, and gain credibility with issuers and investors.

As the market grew, it became harder to match the demands of borrowers with that of investors using the traditional FRN structure. In this context, traditional refers to FRNs with five to 10 years to maturity, and coupons set over Libor and adjusted every three or six months to reflect prevailing interest rates, and which rank as senior obligations of the issuer in the event of a default. Generally-speaking, the market price for FRNs with this structure, issued by prime name borrowers should, at the coupon reset date, be no less than the original purchase price after adjusting for any negative or positive carry. This excludes technical and credit considerations such as over-supply, or a deterioration in the credit quality of the borrower. Events of this nature would adversely affect the price of any security, be it an FRN or fixed-rate eurobond.

As the market grew, therefore, so did the number and complexity of new issues. Secondary market turnover reached unprecedented levels—which, in itself, is fine—except that in this case, market participants lacked the experience both to evaluate and trade effectively the myriad of FRN instruments that came into existence.

In the run-up to the crash, the market became saturated with new, but unsellable, primary issues. Many houses were also long a lot of paper in the secondary market. At about the same time, investors started to examine their FRN investments more closely and realized, albeit too late, the inferior nature of some of their holdings. This was especially the case with certain perpetual notes, of which many billions had by this time been issued. As they rushed to sell, bids disappeared, and widespread panic ensued.

Timetable of events

■ 1980
Market outstandings totalled approximately US$10 billion. The standard spread between bid and offer was 50bp. The average margin over Libor was 25bp, and maturities ranged between five and 10 years. The main issuers were commercial banks, and some LDC sovereign and quasi-sovereign entities such as Argentina, Nafinsa and Pemex. There were approximately eight houses operating as market-makers. The main investors were banks which borrowed funds in the interbank market at or around Libor, and used the money to buy FRNs that yielded more than Libor, thereby earning the spread between the two. These types of investors were thus known as *spread bankers* or *funded investors*. Because FRNs resemble syndicated loans but are more liquid and can be purchased in smaller amounts, they were—and still are—good alternative assets for banks.

■ Late 1982
Mexico defaulted, triggering the LDC debt crisis. This caused a run on US banks exposed to South America, as depositors sought to retrieve their money. This, in turn, caused a surge in the Libor rate (the rate at which banks lend money to each other). A sharp downward revision in the price of FRNs issued by US banks, LDCs and related entities followed.

As a matter of interest, US domestic FRNs, which are largely issued by banks, but pegged to US Treasury bills, came under even worse selling pressure as the 'TED' spread (the spread between US T-bills and Libor) widened to around 4% (400bp)! During this extremely volatile time, the FRN trading community learned an awful lot, but it was still very small. Had there been more FRN traders in 1986 who had traded through the debt crisis in 1982, the collapse may not have happened but, by then, those who remembered the debt crisis were outnumbered by those who did not, by about 10 to 1.

■ 1983-86

This was a period of unprecedented growth, as a variety of quality borrowers, including sovereigns, sovereign-backed entities and prime name global and regional commercial banks, started using the FRN market to raise money. They did this in preference to the syndicated loan market, because of the relatively low cost at which they could raise vast amounts. The investor base also broadened considerably as FRNs became acceptable substitutes for short-dated instruments among money market investors. Fixed investors, attracted by the liquidity, price stability, and issuer quality of FRNs, also used the market as a safe haven during times of interest rate uncertainty. Thus, investors now included a variety of international banks, fund managers, corporations, pension funds and insurance companies.

For quite a while, the market only went up and everyone was happy, especially as FRNs provided capital gain as well as limited downside. But as we know, all good things come to an end. Eventually, margins over Libor declined to the point where some investor groups, spread bankers for example, were unable to participate because the margins over Libor they required were not available. A supply problem was developing, not helped by the fact that more and more prime name borrowers could often achieve lower floating-rate funding through the IRS market.

The Street became very concerned. Certain investor and borrower groups were fading from the market. To attract them back, the Street had to find ways to match the supply and demand of both borrowers and investors. Investors wanted FRNs offering a margin over Libor while borrowers only wanted to issue FRNs at sub-Libor rates.

The old saying that desperation breeds inspiration certainly proved to be the case during this phase. The Street set to work to create new structures that were cost effective for borrowers but also offered sufficiently high yields to investors. The result was a proliferation of FRNs with more complex and/or weaker structures. A variety of new, but lesser quality, borrowers were also encouraged to issue FRNs. The culmination of the Street's efforts was the quasi-equity perpetual floating-rate note, which ultimately proved to be the straw that broke the camel's back.

New FRN structures created during the boom issuing and investing period (1983-86) included:

- Mismatch notes where, for example, coupons reset monthly but in relation to six-month Libor, but pay interest monthly or semi-annually;
- Mismatch notes with protection where coupons reset at the higher of, for example, six-month or one-month Libor;

- Mini-Max notes comprising a cap and a floor on coupon payments;
- Step-up and step-down notes where the spread in relation to Libor increases or decreases at a given point during the life of the note;
- Capped and deferred cap notes where coupons are capped, either for the whole, or a part of a note's life;
- Collateralized notes, some of which contained embedded options such as caps and floors. These are notes collateralized with, for example, mortgages or a portfolio of securities (the income from which is used for interest payments and principal repayment);
- Perpetuals notes, i.e. notes that never mature (!);
- Quasi-equity perpetuals. These are notes with as much as 99 years until maturity, with coupon payments contingent upon dividend payments to stockholders. For example, if an issuer reduces their dividend payments by 50%, then the coupon payment on their perpetual FRNs is reduced by the same percentage. One bank that issued an FRN with this structure in 1986, actually passed a dividend in 1982!

■ Early 1986

Market outstandings now totalled approximately US$150 billion. The spread between bid and offer had narrowed to between 3bp and 10bp. Maturities had extended to eternity, and yield levels were around Libid minus $\frac{1}{16}$% for prime-name FRNs with a conventional structure, up to Libor plus $\frac{3}{16}$% for perpetuals. By this time, there were about fifty houses operating as market-makers.

■ Late 1986

Massive over-supply, and virtually no demand, created panic as professionals sought to sell vast amounts of unsold primary as well as secondary paper ahead of the Christmas holidays. At the same time, Japanese investors were trying to liquidate significant amounts of perpetual notes.[1] Issuance of quasi-equity perpetual debt for lesser grade names however, continued, as firms competed for a higher place in the primary market league tables for the year. There were also a lot of CMO issues on offer in Europe (CMOs are US government-backed FRNs collateralized by mortgage obligations). As these instruments offered higher yields, they

---

[1] *Prompted by concern from the BIS about the capital adequacy of banks, the Japanese Ministry of Finance became particularly concerned about Japanese bank holdings of perpetual FRNs. Fearing they could be forced to stake equity to the value of any perpetual FRN investment, which would have made these holdings much less attractive, Japanese banks became aggressive sellers. As they were the largest holders of perpetuals, the sector suffered meltdown as a result.*

were more attractive for investors looking for floating-rate assets. One-way selling ensued, the majority of dealers ran for cover, and the market collapsed. The underlying fragility of the market was exposed and the confidence of investors was shattered.

Consequences

- Severe losses sustained by both the Street and investors.
- Savage contraction of the market. Numerous job losses.
- Liquidity severely reduced. One of the largest sectors of the eurobond market shattered. Buying power eroded due to vast amounts being tied up in unsellable primary and secondary bonds.

Conclusions

- A coherent and well-thought-out strategy is vital when committing huge amounts of capital to businesses in which you have no prior experience. So is a thorough understanding of how to evaluate the particular instruments to be traded.
- Liquidity disappears in the absence of investor demand. A market cannot thrive unless there are a sufficient number of investors for its product.
- It is extremely difficult to get competitors to pull together, particularly where a big divergence in skills and experience exist.
- When critical decisions are needed, primitive instincts usually dictate the course of action.

Cautionary note

Unless demand is seen to be coming directly from both borrowers and investors, the chances are that it is greatly exaggerated or, worse still, does not exist at all!

What went wrong?

Simply stated, the market collapsed because it grew too quickly and many market-makers were operating with virtually no other resources outside their capital, much of which was understandably lost. The need for product and credit analysts to assess value properly went unnoticed. The need for corporate finance and distribution teams to buy and sell the product direct was ignored. Above all, many of the individuals hired to trade FRNs, lacked the necessary skills and experience.

For quite a while, the market only went up. As a result, many more houses joined the professional arena as market-makers. The majority of newcomers, however, did not understand that markets could actually go down. Indeed, many traders were so young and/or inexperienced, that they had never seen a market go down. As new market-making firms invariably acquired some inventory from which to commence trading (trading from a flat book appeared to be an unknown concept), there was an illusion of demand.

Although investor demand had been steadily increasing in prior years, it had abated considerably in the months leading up the crash. However, only the few houses with direct access to investors knew this. Many houses continued, therefore, to bring ill-structured and/or expensively-priced new issues to the market in the expectation that prices would continue to rise and bail them out of their positions. This had proven to be a successful strategy in the past.

It should also be noted, that many investors contributed to the collapse. They abandoned caution in their quest for yield, and dealt with whichever house offered the cheapest price. Although there were numerous trading opportunities during the crisis, very few investors took advantage of them. They were paralysed with fear. Too few understood the creditworthiness and/or the structure of the various instruments in which they had been investing. Many had simply bought on the assumption that, since everyone else was buying and prices were rising, the assets must be okay. Very few did their own homework and simply rode on the back of those who had. The old market rule of *caveat emptor* (buyer beware) had long been forgotten.

The Ecu bond market collapse 1992

In many ways, the Ecu bond market crisis was a repeat of the FRN debacle, with a few differences. Again, I believe too many houses viewed the Ecu bond market as a relatively cheap and easy way to raise their profiles and gain credibility with issuers and investors. The Street ran ahead of itself on untenable assumptions and purported investor activity, without solid evidence of investor flows. When the complexion of things changed dramatically following the Danish 'No' vote, widespread panic set in.

Timetable of events

■ Mid-1980s
The Ecu bond market developed as a 'retail' sector, with special attractions to Benelux investors, and became an important sub-sector of the eurobond markets.

■ Late 1980s
Development of institutional investor interest, resulting in new 'jumbo' issues. January 1990 saw the launch by the EIB of an Ecu 500mm eurobond, the largest to date.

■ 1991
Significant increase in institutional participation and Ecu jumbos.

■ December 1991
Signing of Maastricht Treaty, with a goal of economic (and, therefore, bond market) convergence and move towards single European currency (Emu). Ecu seen as forerunner of new European currency. Ecu bonds trade at a positive spread (higher yield) than underlying theoretical bond.

■ April 1992
Disillusionment sets in due to poor performance of underlying bond markets. Because of large inventories among professionals, prices of Ecu bonds did not fall sufficiently to maintain a positive spread to underlying theoretical bond. Institutions started selling, but supply not easily absorbed due to professionals being long already and there being insufficient retail demand to mop up the supply. New issue activity dries up.

■ June 1992
Danish (2 June) and Irish (18 June) referenda on Maastricht Treaty. Danes say 'No', denting the smooth track towards Emu, etc.

■ July 1992
In wake of Danish 'No', the Ecu market 'grinds to a halt' (in the words of the Financial Times). At quoted market levels, Ecu bonds now yield less than underlying theoretical bond.

■ 24 July 1992
Ecu bond market-makers relieved of duty to make markets by ISMA, the market's self-regulatory organization.

■ 28 July 1992
Market re-opens with smaller lots and wider bid/offer spreads.

■ Late August 1992
Market suffers second paralysis as dealers protect their bottom line, grinding to a halt by the end of August when, as the FT says, 'liquidity evaporated'. Bid/offer spreads widen to 50bp. Rallies seen only as selling opportunities.

■ 20 September 1992
French referendum on Maastricht. A small 'Yes'.

Consequences

- Severe losses sustained by the Street and investors as a result of substantial inventories purchased at much higher prices.
- Savage contraction of activity in Ecu sector (it had still not recovered after two years). Liquidity severely reduced and jobs lost.

Conclusions

- There is a risk of financial suicide when committing capital based more on expectation and assumption than fact. The Ecu market grew on perceptions of European unification which, although likely, was unrealistic in the short term.
- Liquidity evaporates fast in the absence of two-way flows.
- It is extremely difficult to get competitors to pull together.

The same cautionary note applies. Unless good two-way turnover is seen from investors directly, it may not exist.

What went wrong?

Investors/dealers did not understand the unique risks inherent in owning Ecu bonds. Ecu bonds require sophisticated valuation techniques that only a few institutions can handle. Even so, origination, syndicate, trading and distribution procedures for Ecu bonds, were the same as for well-developed markets.

Unlike other eurobond markets, there is no single 'real' benchmark (i.e. currency and government market) to support Ecu bonds—just a theoretical bond made up of a basket of currencies. Consequently, prices and yields could go anywhere as there is no backstop. If the price of a US$ eurobond for example, were to fall dramatically for no good reason, there would be a point at which it would represent value to certain investors if only as a 'currency play' or core holding. The same is not true for Ecu bonds.

The Ecu bond market was not traditionally a liquid market. Traditional (retail) investors buy in small quantities, and new issues need significant time to become placed and seasoned. Rapid growth in the market outgrew genuine placement. When institutions became disenchanted there were no obvious backstops.

The quality and commitment of secondary dealers was very poor, and too many operated more on assumptions than hard facts. Despite numerous trading opportunities during the ensuing crisis, the majority of investors and dealers were too scared to trade for fear of getting it wrong.

Epilogue

It was not my plan to end this book on a note about disasters, but they do illustrate the magnitude of risk taken by some Street firms.

In 1995 alone, Daiwa Bank, New York sustained a loss in the region of $700 million as a result of an accumulation of dishonest dealings in US government securities by Mr. Toshihide Iguchi. Nick Leeson lost £350 million trading stock index derivatives for Barings, an amount that escalated to £800 million. It broke the bank by the time the various transactions were unwound. The losses in both cases were astronomical in the extreme.

However appalling these situations may seem, though, had adequate supervision and procedures existed within these organizations, trading violations would not have been possible to commit in the first place. Acts of incompetence, greed and dishonesty can occur at all levels, and, regardless of education or experience. Mr. Iguchi was well-educated and experienced, Leeson moderately so, and their various superiors, presumably far more so.

Moreover, rogues and rogue traders will always exist. It would be unrealistic, given the size of the securities industry, to think that it will ever be totally free of people with a tendency to bend the rules and exploit loopholes, given the chance. Therefore, and to reiterate, we all have an obligation to look out for each other. Bland, or hard-to-follow explanations should always be investigated. There are extremely few geniuses in this world. Do not underestimate your powers of perception or your ability to understand plain English. If something sounds too good to be true, it probably *is* too good to be true and, if an individual's profitability seems amazing, a close examination may well reveal exaggerations, blatant misrepresentation of the facts, or exploitation of accounting/reporting systems. Trust your instinct and do not be afraid to ask questions for fear of looking foolish.

The securities industry is like any other. It has to be regulated—and populated—by competent people, who, regardless of seniority, respect its rules and regulations at all times and have the courage to investigate the dubious and report anything untoward.

Glossary

accrued, accrued interest
The build up of interest between interest payment dates.

actual/360 or 365
Refers to interest payments calculated, based on actual days lapsed divided by either 360 or 365 days.

all-in cost
Refers to the cost of raising money to an issuer. A borrower's all in costs are usually expressed as an interest rate and usually includes interest payments and fees/commissions but not listing and other issuing expenses, such as legal fees.

allotment
Allocation of new securities to syndicate members.

arbitrage
To arbitrage is to buy and sell the same or similar securities to take advantage of price discrepancies.

as 'principal'
When a firm takes a position using its own capital, it is acting as principal.

bankers' acceptances
Bills of exchange that are 'accepted' and, therefore guaranteed by, a bank or trust company. A type of guarantee of business done with manufacturers and exporters, but not yet paid for, which they in turn pledge to a bank as collateral in return for a percentage of face value, to avoid cashflow problems and enable them to continue doing business.

basis point (bp)
1/100th of one per cent. Commonly used in the business in terms of both price and yield.

bearer
The name of the owner of a 'bearer' bond is not registered, i.e. does not appear anywhere on the certificate that represents ownership. Bearer bond certificates are issued with interest coupons attached, which owners clip off and simply present for payment. Coupons are therefore paid to the 'bearer' of a coupon.

bearish
Pessimistic on the market, expecting prices to go lower.

benchmark
A base upon which the yield or price of a security is determined. For example, an FRN may pay interest at the rate of 6-month Libor + 20bp and a new issue may be priced to offer a yield above or below US government securities, in which case Libor and US government bonds would represent benchmarks.

bid
Buying price. The price at which a trader will buy.

bond
Technically known as a 'certificate of indebtedness' or debt instrument, because it is a debt obligation of the issuer (borrowing entity). Bond, issue, deal and security are synonymous terms and therefore interchangeable in 'Street speak', e.g., when requesting a price for a bond issued by Marks & Spencer one might say: "Where is the M & S bond?"; "How is the M & S deal?"; "Where is the M & S issue trading?"; "What is the price of the M & S security?". One would of course qualify this further if there were two or more securities outstanding.

bond switch
The sale of one bond and the purchase of another, usually for an increase in yield or improvement in quality or structure.

broker, broke (to)
A broker firm intermediates between buyers and sellers but does not use its own capital to take positions. Although dealers are sometimes called brokers, *to broke* securities means, technically-speaking, to buy from one party and sell to another simultaneously for a small profit (a brokerage fee, also called a *turn*), without taking any market risk.

bullish
Optimistic on the market, expecting prices to go higher.

Bund
An abbreviation for *Bundesobligationen,* i.e. a debt obligation of the German Government.

cap
Refers to interest payments; an upper limit or ceiling on the coupon interest payments on a security. Sometimes a cap may only be in force for a certain period during a bond's life, rather than for the whole of it.

CD
Certificate of deposit. Issued by commercial banks against money held on deposit.

Cedel
Based in Luxembourg, Cedel is one of the two large clearing agents for international securities. The other is Euroclear, which is based in Brussels.

clearance
The exchange of securities for cash, or vice versa, in completion of a trade. Also known as settlement.

CMO
Collateralized mortgage obligation, i.e. a debt security that is backed by a pool of mortgages which are the source of all interest payments and principal repayment.

colour
Another term for information. To give colour on a market is to provide information about what is going on.

commercial paper
Unsecured short-term (less than one year) obligations, issued mostly by corporations and financial organizations.

commodity
A natural resource such as food produce or precious metals/stones.

counterparty
The person or entity with whom you deal and who therefore represents the opposite part of a transaction, i.e. the 'other side' of a trade.

coupon
The rate of interest payable on a security by the issuer.

cover
The next best price.

CRD
Council of Reporting Dealers (an arm of ISMA)

'dead' money
Money on which no interest is being earned.

dealing price
The price at which one can buy or sell.

'deal on the wire'
If a client is ready to 'deal on the wire' it means they are in a position to make a decision to buy or sell at that particular moment, and without the need to put down the telephone.

debt
Debt obligation, the technical term for a bond. *See also* **bond**.

derivative market
The market for financial products which are based on other products and/or markets, having been 'derived' from them. These include futures, options and warrants. A derivative instrument is always based on some other underlying security or market and cannot exist independently.

dirty price
See **full price**.

DSL
Dutch State Loan, i.e. a debt obligation of the Dutch Government.

DTB
Deutsche Terminbörse, the Frankfurt exchange where financial futures are traded.

duration
A measurement of a security's volatility. The percentage price move of a security for a given change in yield.

Ecu
European currency unit. A unit of exchange based on a basket of European currencies which is set to become the common currency for Europe.

Emu
European Monetary Union.

ERM
Exchange rate mechanism, a system via which exchange rates between two or more currencies is controlled by the respective central banks.

Euroclear
See **Cedel**.

execution
Completion of a transaction. i.e. if a client places an order to buy a specific amount of a specific security, when the trader completes the order, he/she will have *executed* the trade and the salesperson will call the client to report an *execution*.

face amount
See **par value**.

face value
The amount written on the face of a bond certificate, i.e. the nominal amount to be repaid at maturity. *See also* **par value**.

Federal Reserve
The central bank of the United States, comprising a collection of banks each of which is responsible for banking activities for a particular district and all of which report to the Federal Reserve Board.

'feel'
A dealer's *feel* is his intuitive and/or intellectual judgement about the direction of prices and yields for his market.

fixed
Fixed-rate securities, where the rate of interest payable to holders is fixed for the life of the instrument. i.e. a bond with a 10 per cent coupon will pay interest at the rate of 10 per cent of face value for each year the bond is outstanding.

fixed currency
Where the exchange rate between two or more currencies is not allowed to move up and down freely but is controlled by a central bank or a group of central banks via a prescribed formula, usually for the purposes of providing economic stability.

floaters
Colloquial term for FRNs.

floor
Refers to interest payments; the minimum interest payable on a security. Often a security is issued with both a cap and floor which means that interest payments will always be within a certain range, regardless of where actual interest rates might be.

FRAs
Forward rate agreements.

free-floating currency
The opposite of the above, where exchange rates move freely based on supply and demand, i.e. the amounts bought and sold relative to other currencies.

FRN
Floating-rate note, so called because the rate of interest payable to holders is adjusted periodically in relation to a benchmark such as Libor.

full price
The net price plus accrued interest, also known as the *gross* or *dirty price*.

fungibility
Where contract specifications and trading and settlement procedures are identical, so that the same contract can be bought on one exchange and sold on another. In the context of bonds, it relates to whether subsequent tranches of an issue are identical and therefore interchangeable with the initial tranche.

futures
An abbreviation for *futures contract*. Futures contracts exist for commodities, currencies and indexes, as well as financial instruments.

gross price
See **full price**.

GTR
An abbreviation for guarantor. Some bond issues are explicitly guaranteed by, for example, a parent company or government. In some cases, a guarantor may be a seemingly unrelated party. Bonds that are not specifically guaranteed are general unsecured obligations of the issuer.

hedge
A trade entered into for the express purpose of protecting existing positions against adverse market movements.

higher repayment ranking
Bonds issued by banks usually rank *pari passu* (equal to) depositors meaning that in the event of a default bondholders will be in the first category of debtors to be repaid.

hit
Term used to describe a (sometimes unwanted) purchase of bonds, e.g. "I've just been hit at 99".

house
A financial institution involved in trading securities as principal and/or broker. *See* **as principal**.

illiquid
Refers to securities that are harder to buy or sell, i.e. bonds for which there are few or no registered market-makers. A bond can become illiquid for a variety of reasons, the most common being a deterioration in the creditworthiness of the issuer.

indication
An indication is an approximate idea of where a security is trading, not a firm price at which one can trade.

'in-syndicate'
When a new issue is in syndicate, it is in the process of being distributed to end-investors by those houses that comprise the syndicate group.

inventory
Securities held in position.

investor
A company/co-operative which purchases or sells bonds for investment rather than speculation. These include pension funds, insurance companies and fund managers. Investors are also referred to as *clients, institutional investors, retail accounts* or simply just *accounts,* or simply just *retail,* although some firms reserve the use of the term 'retail' to describe individual, rather than institutional, investors.

IPMA
International Primary Markets Association.

ISMA
International Securities Market Association, formerly AIBD (Association of International Bond Dealers).

issuer(s)
Borrower(s). Entities that raise money in the markets by issuing securities such as shares or bonds.

key issue(s)
The most recently issued government bonds in the US domestic market. These are often used as benchmarks for assessing value on other similarly-structured securities.

LDC
Less-developed countries, now known as *emerging* economies, which is less derogatory.

league-table
See subsection 'League tables' in Chapter 9.

Libid
London interbank bid rate, i.e. the rate at which banks will buy money from other banks; what they will pay for deposits of money.

Libor
London interbank offered rate, i.e. the rate at which banks will lend (offer) money to other banks.

LIFFE
London International Financial Futures & Options Exchange, the London exchange where financial futures are traded.

lifted/taken/lost
Terms used to describe a sale of bonds. If a dealer says "I've just been lifted", he means he has just made a price (a market) and that his counterparty (which could be a competitor or a client) has dealt on his offering price and has purchased securities from him.

liquidate
Term to describe a position in security that has been extinguished, i.e. bought or sold resulting in no position and therefore liquidated.

liquidity
Ease of tradeability of a security, i.e. the ease with which a security can be bought or sold. If there are a lot of dealers in a particular bond, then it is considered to be very liquid. If there are none, it would be illiquid.

liquidity upside
A bond's potential to become more actively traded and therefore easier to buy and sell.

long-dated FRN
FRNs with longer maturities relative to what is regarded by the market as normal. This can change.

M & A
Mergers and acquisitions.

make a market
To provide both a bid price and an offer price in a security. If a dealer, when asked for a market, responds, "99 bid", he is only providing a one-way market. A market usually comprises a two-way price, i.e. both a bid and an offer.

mandate
A binding instruction to proceed, as in a borrower giving formal notice to a house that they have been awarded the mandate to lead manage their new issue.

market
The eurobond market and the stock market are umbrella terms under which fall the trading of a variety of securities. If you ask a dealer in US dollar-denominated eurobonds, "What's the market doing?", your question would relate to the major bond market influencing the US dollar eurobond market, which would be the US government bond market. If you asked, "What's your market doing?", then the enquiry would relate to the dollar eurobond market and, more specifically, the particular sector of the market he trades.

market risk
Refers to the risk of a market going up or down as a result of movements in interest rates and/or changes in supply and demand.

MATIF
Marché à Terme International de France, the Paris exchange where financial futures are traded.

maturity
The date when a security matures and is redeemed by the issuer, i.e. when owners receive back their principal and any interest still owing to them.

maturity date
The date when a loan or security becomes due for redemption.

mm
Abbreviation for million.

money market
As well as referring to the various markets that deal with deposits and loans of cash, this is the general term used to describe markets in short-dated securities which are substitutes for cash.

'...more behind'
Refers to whether a client or competitor has more business to do in a security beyond what they have divulged.

MTN
Medium-term note.

net price
The price of a bond net of accrued interest.

notional bond
Theoretical bond.

offer
Offering price. The price at which a trader will sell.

'off market' swap
A swap involving odd amounts. In the context of bonds, *off-market* can refer to a price that is wrong, or to a switch transaction where the prices of the respective securities are marked up or down and do not, therefore, reflect

the prices where business can legitimately be done. Note, however, that firms are legally required to trade at prices prevailing at the time of execution.

offshore
Not domestic or home-based, i.e. markets or funds which are outside the country of the currency in question.

on-lend
Refers to securities or funds that are borrowed and then loaned to another entity/person.

OPEC
Oil Producing Exporting Countries.

OTC
An abbreviation for *over-the-counter*, i.e. the trading of securities that does not take place via a public exchange, such as the London Stock Exchange. OTC securities, which are usually traded by telephone or electronic screen, are not subject to the standardization of exchange-traded contracts and, in many cases, their terms may be negotiated by the parties to the trade.

outright or on swap
Refers to whether a client is buying or selling securities outright with new cash or because they need cash, or whether another transaction is involved. It is important to know where money is coming from and where it is going as it may represent another trading opportunity.

overhanging
An abbreviation for *overhanging the Street*, i.e. when large amounts of securities are still in professional hands and yet to be distributed to investors.

P+L
Profit and loss.

par bond
A bond that is trading at or close to 100 per cent of face value.

partial delivery
The delivery of a portion, but not all, of the securities contracted to be delivered. A partial delivery can be refused by the buyer unless partial delivery was agreed at the time of execution.

partials
Relates to whether or not a counterparty will accept a partial execution, i.e. would they be happy to just buy two million bonds even though they would prefer to buy five million, or is there order/interest on an 'all or none' basis.

par value
Par or *face* value is the principal amount (value) that appears on the face of a bond certificate and upon which interest is calculated. Bonds are usually issued in denominations (with a face value) of 1000 or multiples thereof. When used in the context of bond prices therefore, par means 100 per cent of a principal amount of 1000 or some multiple of it. This is the amount that will be repaid at maturity. Also note that, while coupons (interest payments) are based on par or face value, a security's real value—the price at which it can be bought or sold at any given point in time—will be a function of market conditions and may be very different from face value. With regard to the stock market, par means the price assigned by a company to its common stock or ordinary shares.

perpetuals
Debt instruments (mostly FRNs) with no maturity, or either a very long maturity, i.e. 99 years.

plain vanilla
A bond with a conventional structure, usually taken to mean a fixed-rate security with a common maturity.

point
One percentage point (100 basis points).

portfolio
The securities held by an individual or institution for investment purposes.

position
long position: To own securities. If a dealer says "I'm long the market", he means that he owns securities, which should mean that he expects prices to go higher.

short position: When a dealer is 'short the market', it means he has sold securities that he does not own, and which he will have to buy back (cover) at some point. Except for hedging purposes, if a short position is established deliberately in a particular security then the dealer would be expecting the price of that security to fall.

flat position: When a dealer is neither long nor short the market on a net basis. For example if a dealer owns (is long) 50,000,000 bonds and is also short 50,000,000 other bonds, he would have a net flat position. A position of 50 million long and 30 million short would equal a net long position of 20 million. To be completely flat is to be neither long nor short in any security.

position securities
The 'positioning' of a security usually means its purchase, rather than a short sale, even though a position can be created through buying or selling.

primary market
The market for new issues.

principal
The face amount, i.e. the initial loan to an issuer, which is repaid at maturity.

proprietary
A firm that acts in a proprietary capacity uses its own capital, i.e. money which belongs to its principals or partners or, in the case of a public corporation, its shareholders.

puts/calls
Many bonds contain a clause which give the issuer the right to 'call' (buy back) some or all of the bonds prior to maturity, usually at certain times which are detailed in the prospectus at the time the issue is launched. A put gives the holder of the security the right to 'put' (sell back) securities to the issuer. Some bonds have both puts and calls, usually exercisable at different times during a bond's life.

rally
A rise in prices.

ramp
When a house buys lots of a security and forces up the price to a level where it has no value relative to other comparable bonds.

rating
A measurement of the perceived financial health and creditworthiness of a company, or country, as supplied by a rating agency. *See* **rating agency.**

rating agency
A company that grades or 'rates' borrowers and/or specific bonds. A rating helps investors assess an issuer's financial health and ability to honour their debt obligations. An AAA (or, a Triple-A) rating means one can be confident that an issuer can meet all interest payments and principal repayment at maturity. However, sometimes an AAA rating is assigned to a specific issue because it is collateralized with top-quality assets from where all interest and principal comes. Standard & Poor's, Moody's and Duff & Phelps are three of the bigger rating agencies. A borrower that is assigned an AAA rating is in excellent financial health whereas one that is assigned a CCC rating is more risky and may not, for example, be in business when its debt obligations mature. Ratings can, and do, change.

redemption
Expiration of a debt obligation, i.e. when a bond matures. An issuer could redeem securities and, in so doing, extinguish debt obligations by buying them in the secondary market prior to the official maturity date. Issuers sometimes do this if their securities are on sale at less than face or redemption value, and if they can afford it.

Registered Dealers
Houses that are registered as market-makers in a security with the Council of Reporting Dealers (CRD) a semi-autonomous arm of ISMA. Registered market-makers are listed in ISMA's directory, which is used by the market professionals and investors to ascertain who to call for a price.

relative value
The appeal of one bond or market relative to another, i.e. to compare one bond against another similar bond to assess its attractiveness. For two bonds to be compared they need to be of similar credit standing and structure.

retail customers
See investor.

Reuters *Abacus*
A computer program, designed and owned by Reuters, which identifies anomalies in the foreign exchange market and thereby opportunities for arbitrage.

Savings & Loans
The US equivalent of UK building societies.

SEC
Securities and Exchange Commission, a regulatory body (USA).

secondary market
The market where securities are traded after their initial launch when they are no longer new issues.

settlement
Settlement is effected when securities and cash in respect of a transaction have been exchanged. *See* **clearance.**

settlement date
See **clearance.**

SFA
The Securities and Futures Authority, a self-regulatory organization (SRO) in the UK.

short-dated FRN
FRNs with short maturities of a few years or less.

SIB
Securities and Investments Board, the head of a group of regulatory bodies set up to regulate investment businesses and to protect investors.

spot
Originated from 'on the spot' meaning to deal now for the most immediate settlement possible, which is usually the day following a transaction.

spot rates
Prices for spot rather than future settlement.

spread
The yield differential between a standard benchmark and a particular security, or two different securities. For example, if the yield between 5-year bonds issued by Chrysler and Ford Motor has been consistent at, say, 50bp but then widened to 100bp, dealers would say that 'the spread has widened'.

squeezed
When unusually large amounts of a security are purchased in an attempt to control the price, then the security is referred to as being squeezed.

Street (The)

Derived from 'Wall Street'. A generic term used to describe the collective business of financial institutions involved in the securities industry, i.e. firms that intermediate between users (borrowers) and lenders (investors) of money, often trading (buying and selling) securities for their own account, as well as on behalf of institutional investors.

subject

Not firm, indicating a need to check before confirming.

subordinated debt

Subordinated debt has a lower repayment ranking. In the event of a default therefore, senior noteholders would be paid before subordinated noteholders. There are also different levels of subordination, particularly among FRN issues. Junior subordinated debt, for example, offers less security of repayment in the event of a default, than subordinated debt.

swap curve

A graphical illustration of swap rates for different periods.

swaps market

Refers to the interest rate and currency swaps markets.

swap rate

In the FX market, the swap rate is the difference between the spot and forward rates at which a currency is traded. In the context of an interest rate swap, it is the fixed rate of interest a dealer will pay or receive in return for a floating rate of interest.

swap/switch

The sale and purchase of two securities. *See* **bond switch**.

syndicate

The launching of a new issue is handled by a firm's Syndicate Department. Syndicate managers are responsible for pricing a new issue. This means that they bear ultimate responsibility for deciding the yield and structure of new issues.

T-bills

Treasury bills. Short-term debt obligations of the US Government.

tick

The minimum price change on a futures contract.

trade date
The date when a transaction is executed.

trader
A person who buys and sells (trades) securities; also called a *dealer* or *market-maker* and sometimes a *broker*.

Treasury yield
The yield of a US government bond.

Triple-A rating
See **rating agency**.

unlisted
Securities, i.e. notes/bonds that are not listed on a designated exchange, such as the London or Luxembourg stock exchange.

unwind
The process of reversing an existing position, either by liquidating or by doing off-setting transactions.

volatility
A measurement of the price movement of a security during a specific period.

well-rated
Refers to securities of good credit quality that are assigned a top rating by one of the big rating agencies. *See* **rating agency.**

write tickets
Street-speak for 'doing business'. A salesperson who writes a lot of tickets is one who does a lot of business.

yield
An abbreviation for *yield-to-maturity*. For a fixed-rate bond, this is the annual rate of return, based on its coupon, maturity and price, expressed as a percentage interest rate.

yield curve
A graphical illustration of yield levels for a particular market.

> **inverted curve:** An inverted curve means that long-term interest rates are lower than short-term interest rates.

'off the curve': When a bond is trading off the curve, it means that it is cheaper (higher-yielding) than the benchmark government bond with the same, or a similar, maturity.

positive curve: A positive curve means that long-term interest rates are higher than short-term interest rates.

'through the curve': When a bond is trading through the curve, it means that it is more expensive (lesser-yielding) than the benchmark government bond with the same, or a similar, maturity.

YTC
An abbreviation for *yield-to-call*. If a bond is callable by the issuer prior to the official maturity date, its yield-to-call may be different from its yield-to-maturity, especially if the call price is significantly different from par.

YTM
yield-to-maturity. *See* **yield**.

zero curve
A graphical illustration of yields for zero-coupon securities for different periods.

Bibliography

- Alman E.I. and Nammacher S.A., *Investing in Junk Bonds: Inside the High Yield Debt Market*. Wiley 1987.

- Battley, Nick, *An Introduction to Commodity Futures & Options*. Irwin Professional Publishing 1995.

- Brett, Michael, *How to Read the Financial Pages: A simple guide to the way money works and the jargon*. Guild Publishing 1989.

- Brown, Patrick J., *Formulae for Yield and Other Calculations*. International Securities Market Association, 1992.

- Evans, Roger and Russell, Peter, *The Creative Manager*. Unwin Paperbacks 1990. Out of print.

- Fisher, F.G. III., *Eurobonds*. Euromoney Publications plc. 1988.

- Fitch, Thomas, *Barron's Dictionary of Banking Terms*. Barron's Educational Series, Inc., 1993.

- Frost, Ronald J., *Options on Futures: A Hands-On Workbook of Market-Proven Trading Strategies*. McGraw-Hill Book Company 1989.

- Homer S. and Leibowitz M.L. PhD., *Inside the Yield Book: New Tools for Bond Market Strategy*. Prentice-Hall and N.Y. Institute of Finance 1972.

- Hull, John., *Introduction To Futures And Options Markets*. Prentice-Hall International Editions 1995.

- IPMA (International Primary Market Association), *Members Recommendations Standard Documentation*. IPMA London 1993.

- ISMA (International Securities Market Association), *Statutes, By-Laws, Rules and Recommendations*. Neidhart + Schön Druck, Zurich 1995.

- Johnston, R.B., *The Economics of the Euro-Market: History, Theory and Policy*. The MacMillan Press Ltd. 1983.

- Kaufman, H., *Interest Rates, The Markets and the New Financial World*. I.B. Tauris & Co. Ltd. 1986.

- Moles, Peter A. and Terry, Nicholas., *Oxford Handbook of International Finance*. Oxford University Press 1995.

- Nelson, Charles R., *The Investor's Guide to Economic Indicators*. John Wiley & Sons 1987.

- New York Institute of Finance. *The Securities Industry Glossary*. NYIF 1985.

- Pessin, Alan H., *Fundamentals of the Securities Industry*. NYIF, a division of Prentice Hall, 1985.

- Securities and Investments Board (SIB) Publications for Investors. The SIB publishes a variety of booklets which are available on request from their Public Information Office (*Telephone*: London, 0171-638-1240. *Address:* Gavrelle House, 2-14 Bunhill Row, London EC1Y 8RA0).

- Shearlock, Peter and Ellington, William, *The Eurobond Diaries*. Euroclear Clearance System Société Coopérative 1994.

- Stigum, Marcia, in collaboration with Mann, John, *Money Market Calculations: Yield, Break-Evens and Arbitrage*. Dow Jones-Irwin 1981.

- Stigum, Marcia, *After the Trade: Dealer and Clearing Bank Operations in Money Market and Government Securities*. Dow Jones-Irwin, Homewood, Illinois 1988.

- Woelfel, Charles J., *The Desktop Guide to Money, Time, Interest and Yields*. Probus Publishing Company, Chicago, Illinois 1986.

The Publisher...

Irwin Professional is a leading international business and finance publishing company, committed to excellence. Our books and information products are known worldwide for their quality and clarity. We are proud to be the publishers of acknowledged experts in the subjects of investments, banking, the capital markets, trading, international securities, accountancy, taxation, property, insurance, sales management, marketing, quality management and healthcare.

Why not forward us your contact information to allow us to send you information about our full range? In addition, we are always interested to hear from potential authors. If you have a project that you believe would compliment our list then please get in touch.

You can contact Irwin Professional at:

Irwin Professional   *OR*   Irwin Professional
1333 Burr Ridge Parkway   Lynton House
Burr Ridge   7-12 Tavistock Square
IL 60521   London WC1H 9LB
USA   England
Tel: (708) 789-4000   Tel: (0171) 388-7676
Tel [Sales]: 800-634-3966 [USA only]   Fax: (0171) 391-6555
Fax: (708) 789-6933

This Book...

Many associations and companies find that Irwin Professional titles make excellent training and marketing tools. Our books are an extremely cost efficient way of giving yourself, your clients and your colleagues, high quality information about a large range of topics in finance and business. If you would like to organize a bulk purchase at a discount from the full list price, or are interested in a customized edition, please contact our offices at the above addresses.

Money Market Derivatives and Structured Notes
Marcia Stigum
368 pages, Irwin Professional, 1996. ISBN 0 7863 0438 3

Marcia Stigum, the best-selling and esteemed author of *The Money Market*, examines the most critical and dynamic area of the money market in the new *Money Market Derivatives and Structured Notes*. Providing the latest information on financial futures, Treasury bond and note futures, options, euros, and interest rate swaps. It includes:

- The mechanics, structures, and evolution of today's popular money market derivatives.
- Money market derivatives hedging strategies.

Frontiers in Fixed Income Management
Thomas S.Y. Ho, Editor
300 pages, Irwin Professional, 1995. ISBN 1 55738 875 X

"Tom Ho continues to define the cutting edge of fixed income analytics. Practitioners will find a number of important new concepts directly applicable to the issues they face." - Stewart Morrison, Vice President, Keyport Life Insurance Co.

Based on presentations made at the Third Annual GAT Fixed Income Conference, the premiere forum for the discussion of advanced topics in the fixed income arena, *Frontiers in Fixed Income Management* reflects the latest thinking and research in the field. Specific topics include:

- Strategic Portfolio Management: Discusses the inadequacy of duration and convexity as risk measures, the use of primitive securities to control duration drift, and utilizing general algorithms to develop dynamic investment strategies.
- CMOs, Whole Loans. and Structured Notes: Highlights include a stochastic evaluation of whole loan credit risk, constructing an in-house adjustable-rate mortgage model, and using pathwise strategies to make strategic asset liability management decisions.
- Credit Risk: This section provides a unique analysis of the term structure of credit spreads.

The Handbook of Fixed Income Securities (Fourth Edition)
Frank J. Fabozzi & T. Dessa Fabozzi, **Editors**
1,400 pages. Irwin Professional, 1994. ISBN 0 7863 0001 9

"We in the fixed income markets almost universally refer to it simply as 'The Handbook'." - Frank J. Jones, PhD, Senior Vice President and Chief Investment Officer, The Guardian Life Insurance Company of America

Over 100,000 copies sold in previous editions! For years, individual and institutional investors have relied on *The Handbook* to help them understand the dynamics and opportunities within the fixed income market. Now, in this completely revised and updated Fourth Edition, Frank Fabozzi and T. Dessa Fabozzi once again assemble the leading authorities in the field to address the latest developments, financial instruments and portfolio strategies. The Fourth Edition introduces 10 new chapters that explore such timely topics as:

- Valuation of bonds with embedded options
- New duration measures for risk management
- Risk measures for foreign bonds
- The management of high-yield bond portfolios
- Treasury bond futures mechanics and basis valuation

Active Total Return Management of Fixed Income Portfolios
(Revised Edition)
Ravi E. Dattatreya & Frank J. Fabozzi
350 pages, Irwin Professional, 1995. ISBN 1 55738 565 3

In the revised edition of this acclaimed classic, Ravi Dattatreya and Frank Fabozzi set forth a framework by which a portfolio manager or trader can identify value and assess risk. The limitations of yield measures, duration, and convexity are clearly illustrated. A new technique for measuring and controlling yield curve risk is presented.

Relying on logical—rather than mathematical—explanations, *Active Total Return Management of Fixed Income Portfolios* is one of the most incisive, up-to-date guides on the latest tools for managing a fixed income portfolio. Specific topics include amongst others:

- The limitations of yield measures
- The drawbacks of duration and convexity as measures of interest rate risk
- The measurement and control of yield curve risk
- Analysis of callable bonds and mortgage-backed securities
- The use of derivative instruments (options, futures, forwards, and swaps) in controlling risk

Advanced Fixed Income Portfolio Management - The State of the Art
Frank J. Fabozzi & Gifford Fong
350 pages, Irwin Professional, 1994. ISBN 1 55738 862 8

"The book is done with typical Fabozzi and Fong depth and breadth. It provides a demonstrative road to higher yields and enhanced portfolio techniques. A capital markets catalyst for keeping in touch with new strategies and profit-making techniques in the fixed income markets." - James J. Kilbane, Vice President, Defined Contribution Plans, Putnam Investments

In *Advanced Fixed Income Portfolio Management*, Frank J. Fabozzi and Gifford Fong thoroughly explain the latest strategies and techniques for investing in the fixed income market. They discuss valuation techniques, active strategies, indexing strategies, immunization strategies and cashflow matching strategies. In addition, they discuss how to measure interest rate and yield curve risk.

Divided into three sections - Sources and Measurement of Risk, Valuation and Portfolio Management Strategies - the book provides answers for portfolio managers seeking to meet the challenge of active management and asset allocation modelling.

Fixed Income Mathematics (Revised Edition)
Frank J. Fabozzi
400 pages, Irwin Professional, 1993. ISBN 1 55738 423 1

"Must reading for both new and experienced bond portfolio managers." - David T. Yuen, Vice President and Portfolio Manager, Franklin Management Inc.

"The mathematical and analytical aspects have become an integral part of the mainstream of the bond markets. Nevertheless, most books on the topic are both unnecessarily complex and fragmented. This is the first book that provides a comprehensive and readily comprehensible approach to 'bond math' and applies these topics to bond market strategies." - Frank J. Jones, PhD., Senior Vice President and Chief Investment Officer, The Guardian Life Insurance Company of America.

Fixed Income Mathematics covers far more than this simple title might suggest: it not only provides the basics of fixed income analysis, but also the more advanced techniques used by the professionals to value the increasingly complex fixed income securities now being traded. For each key concept, this working reference provides in-depth coverage of the mathematical techniques available as well as specific applications for their use in real-world investment decision-making situations.

Fixed Income Investment - Recent Research
Thomas S.Y. Ho, Editor
312 pages, Irwin Professional, 1994. ISBN 0 7863 0268 2

Fixed Income Investment brings you the recent research about fixed income securities, including advances in investment technologies. Managers of investment portfolios and asset/liability managers will find these insights eminently useful in today's volatile investment climate.

Fixed Income Investment examines the latest risk valuation and analysis techniques as well as newapproaches to structured portfolio management.

Topics covered include:

- Stochastic models of prepayments along interest rate paths
- Decomposition of option-embedded securities into their 'primitive' parts
- Bond dynamic hedging using a return attribution system
- Optimization techniques combined with stochastic horizon analysis
- A consistent framework for evaluating corporate debt and equity
- How pathwise immunization helps standardize the behaviour of portfolios under different interest rate scenarios

---

The European Bond Markets (6th Edition)
The EFFAS European Bond Commission
1700 pages Irwin Professional, 1996. ISBN 1 900717 02 6

This long-awaited 6th Edition has new sections and extended coverage, including Israel, Hungary, the Czech Republic, Slovakia, Bulgaria, Turkey and Russia. It continues to be a leading reference work about the European debt markets, containing the detailed knowledge and expertise of Europe's most important financial institutions.

This edition also retains its user friendly, country-by-country format, with additional articles of key interest to market users. In addition, a special chapter on bond mechanics enables readers to digest and compare yield calculation information between markets.

The Fabozzi Library for Institutional Investment

Bond Portfolio Management *Frank J. Fabozzi*
512 pages, Irwin Professional, 1996
ISBN 1 883249 08 2

CMO Portfolio Management *Frank J. Fabozzi*
325 pages, Irwin Professional, 1996
ISBN 1 883249 01 5

Whole-Loan CMOs
Frank J. Fabozzi, Chuck Ramsey and Frank R. Ramirez, Editors
297 pages, Irwin Professional, 1996
ISBN 1 883249 04 X

Corporate Bonds - Structures & Analysis
Richard S. Wilson and Frank J. Fabozzi
375 pages, Irwin Professional, 1996
ISBN 1 883249 07 4

The Handbook of Equity Style Management
T. Daniel Coggin and Frank J. Fabozzi, Editors
270 pages, Irwin Professional, 1996
ISBN 1 883249 05 8

Collateralized Mortgage Obligations - Structures and Analysis
Revised Edition *Frank J. Fabozzi*
Chuck Ramsey and Frank R. Ramirez
267 pages, Irwin Professional, 1996
ISBN1 883249 03 1

Valuation of Fixed Income Securities and Derivatives *Frank J. Fabozzi*
260 pages, Irwin Professional 1996
ISBN 1 883249 06 6